The 5000 BEST Sale & Promotional Names & Ideas

Ever Compiled

EDITION I

The 5000 BEST Sale & Promotional Names & Ideas Ever Compiled

EDITION I

By

RICK SEGEL

Specific
House
PUBLISHING

The 5000 Best Sale & Promotional Names & Ideas Ever Compiled

Edition I

Published by:

Specific House PUBLISHING   Specific House Publishing
543 Davinci Pass
Poinciana, FL 34759

Requests for permission should be sent to:

Specific House Publishing
543 Davinci Pass
Poinciana, FL 34759
781.272.9995
800.847.9411 (fax)

Printed in the United States of America

ISBN 0-9674586-5-X

Table of Contents

Dedication

This book is about words. The right words at the right time that can make a difference in a sale, a promotion, or a business. But the right words can make a difference in someone's life as well. So although this is a business resource tool, I want to dedicate it to part of my business resource tools, three of my dearest friends.

To my oldest and closet friend, Larry Lyons, who is the brightest person I have ever known. We have been friends for 40 years and he is the best friend any man could ever have. He is always there for me and has given me the best advice anyone can ever get. Sorry I'm not dedicating a great steamy novel but it's the best I can do for now. Stay healthy!

To another 40 year old friend Maxene Rosenthal, who is the best conversationalist in the world. She always knows the right words. So it's only appropriate that this book be dedicated to her. (She is also one of the most knowledgeable sports fans I have ever met.) She communicates well but she listens even better. That's why everybody loves her and she has more friends than anyone else I know. She has listened to more of my crazy ideas over the years than anyone else. Thanks for not being judgmental and always being diplomatic. I sincerely appreciate our friendship.

Lastly, I want to dedicate this book to Darren LaCroix, a partner, a friend, a mentee, and a mentor. It's not often when the student becomes your teacher. Darren won the International Toastmasters speaking competition in 2001 and I have been privileged to watch his career explode. He is truly a man of words and I am honored to be referred to as your friend. You are the Champion.

Acknowledgments

There are always people behind every project. They are the people who made this book a reality. This is the place where I get to officially thank them. They all know how important they are to me, but now I can reveal their behind the scene status. To Cynthia Potts, the best editor and researcher any writer could have. She keeps me motivated by always uncovering the unique and different. I will probably never do another project without her.

To Jim and Barbara Weems from Ad Graphics whom I absolutely drive crazy. You are wonderful and have the patience of Job. Thanks guys. A special thanks to Melody Morris from Central Plains, another great job. To my wife Margie, who is involved in every project I do. I couldn't do it without you. You are a great partner and advisor. Lastly, I want to thank the crew at Specific House Publishing for running with the idea and making it come alive.

THE 5000 BEST SALE & PROMOTIONAL NAMES & IDEAS EVER COMPILED

EDITION I

***

Introduction

& How To Use This Book

I lied! That's not the best way to start an introduction but I have to get it off my chest before we begin. There are more than 5,000 names, titles, events, and ideas for running almost any kind of sale or promotion you could ever want to have. Actually, there are 5638 entries BUT *The 5000 Best Sale and Promotional Names and Ideas Ever Compiled* sounded much better and the title works. After all you bought it or at least it intrigued you enough to be reading this book. Having the right title can make a difference just as 75% Off is a great Sale term but Half of Half sounds even better and gives the same discount.

A Sidewalk Sale is a classic. It just works. Why? Originally because it was different but eventually it created a brand of its own. A Sidewalk Sale represents the deepest of discounts. Shakespeare wrote, "What's in a name?" Juliet said that it didn't matter. Well Juliet wasn't planning a sale or promotion. When it comes to a sale, the name is everything!

The right name can define your business. The right name can build a tradition. The wrong name is never remembered. While we talk about building a tradition, understand that this book is not just about looking for a title and using it. Certainly that will happen and that's great. However, the real benefit of this book is serving as a spring board for ideas of your own. Many of the titles can be combined which creates an infinite amount of possibilities.

We have structured this book where my 50 favorite titles are in the first chapter. Then I explain my Misery Meter Concept. In short, it means that the more miserable a customer thinks you are, the more they will attend a sale event. On one end of the meter is the 5% off Sale and the extreme other end is the Going Out of Business Sale. We have classified all of the Sale events between the numbers 1 through 4 to help you decide what type of title to employ. Then, we breakdown the calendar by month and recommend the best title to use and when.

We have also included celebrities' birthdays, events, and various holidays to celebrate. Many of the listings came from *Chases Calendar of Events*, published by McGraw Hill. We don't go into any detail with the various listings and we urge you to either buy *Chases Calendar of Events* or go to your public library to get more information about the event. There is also contact information in Chases that can be invaluable.

I once bought too much leopard for my apparel store, but instead of having a Leopard Sale I celebrated National Wildlife Week and the sponsoring organization sent free posters and press releases. We sold out almost to the piece at regular price. Obviously, I have only selected events that have some type of retail connection but you might have a tie in that I missed – so check out the book.

There are certain celebrities who sell merchandise very well, such as Elvis and Martha Stewart and their birthdays always make for great promotions. I also strongly recommend you submit your events to Chases. It doesn't cost and can help to make your event an even bigger success. Yes, create your own holiday, celebrate your own week, or create a new promotion while creating your tradition.

We have added one more feature to this book that will help you in selecting an event. We have added a small box beside each name to check off as you are reading. There is no need to underline or highlight – just check your favorite. Lastly, I have decided to offer a free monthly update of new sale terms. Just email your name and place Sale Terms in the subject line and I will place you on our automatic update. If you have any terms that you would like to share, please pass them along and we will add them to the list. We plan on annually updating this book.

Rick's Fab 50

*O*kay, so the more than 5000 suggestions you're holding in your hand are too many to go through quickly. You need something right now – or better, yesterday! I can't time travel for you, but I do have a list of 50 great ideas that you can use immediately. I call them my Fab 50.

This short list is intended as a quick reference of Sale ideas but hopefully it will inspire you to create your own Sale names. Take note – some of the names (like Bankruptcy and Going Out Of Business) have laws written about their use. Check with your local chamber of commerce or small business association to make sure you are able to use the terms.

Many of the names are Mix-and-match, so if the name feels a little light try adding another Fab 50 name and see if it feels better for you. For instance, Combine a "% Off" an "Everything In The Store" and a "Moving Sale" to get "50% Off Everything In The Store Moving Sale."

❑ Buy One Get One Free

❑ Oops We Goofed Sale

❑ Season Ending Sale

❑ Over Stocked and Over Stocked

❑ The Must Attend Sale

❑ Manager's Sale

❑ Buy One Second One Free

❑ Customer Appreciation

- ❏ Grand Opening
- ❏ Sidewalk Sale
- ❏ Sale of Sales
- ❏ Mega Sale
- ❏ The Sale of All Sales
- ❏ Liquidation
- ❏ Forced to Liquidate
- ❏ (reason to) Liquidate
- ❏ Warehouse Liquidation
- ❏ Forced to Sell
- ❏ Cash Raising Sale
- ❏ Cash Raising Event
- ❏ Out of Space Sale
- ❏ Need Room Sale
- ❏ (Holiday) Sale
- ❏ Limited Time Sale
- ❏ Going Out of Business
- ❏ Big Top Sale
- ❏ Off Season Sale
- ❏ Bargain Bin Sale
- ❏ Moving Sale
- ❏ Pre-Moving Sale
- ❏ Wall-To-Wall Sale
- ❏ Total Liquidation
- ❏ Last Blast Sale
- ❏ Free Financing
- ❏ __% Off Sale
- ❏ Early Bird
- ❏ Everything in the Store
- ❏ We Love (Brand) Sale
- ❏ Truckload Sale
- ❏ Free Gift With Purchase
- ❏ Gigantic Store Closing Sale
- ❏ Floor Model Sale
- ❏ Discontinued Merchandise
- ❏ (Year) Anniversary Sale
- ❏ Scratch & Dent Sale
- ❏ One Day Only Sale
- ❏ Shipped Too Late For _____
- ❏ Warehouse Sale
- ❏ 7 Day Coupon Sale
- ❏ Bargain of the Month
- ❏ Overstock Sale
- ❏ Annual Clearance Sale

- ❏ Buy Two Get One Free
- ❏ Back Room Sale
- ❏ Invitation Only Sale
- ❏ President's Gift Certificate
- ❏ Club Members Only
- ❏ Bankruptcy Sale
- ❏ Ticket To Savings Sale
- ❏ Going, Going, Gone!
- ❏ End of Model Year Sale

- ❏ Biggest. Sale. Ever.
- ❏ Nine to Five Sale
- ❏ Last Chance to Save Sale
- ❏ (Color) Tag Sale
- ❏ Midnight Madness
- ❏ Extra Discounts on Already Reduced Merchandise
- ❏ Factory Authorized/ Unauthorized Sale

Ranking the Type of Event & Understanding the Misery Meter

*H*ow to use the SALE TERMS section: I have provided over 2000 unique terms that you can use to help promote your sales. I encourage you to combine these names with the other sections, like Months, Weeks, Days, Birthdays, or Events.

For example, you can combine a "50 Percent Off Sale" with a birthday or event to make "Washington's Birthday Sale-a-bration – 50% Off Sale" – bringing together three different terms (two Sales Terms and one Birthday) to make your event. Be creative!

Understanding the Misery Meter

People love disasters. If you've ever been stuck in traffic because of an accident ahead of the road, you know that in most situations, the delay is not caused by road obstruction, but by curiosity – people slowing down to see what happened and to whom.

In running a good sale, retailers should play off of this natural curiosity in humans by giving people a disaster that will benefit their budget.

One of the basic rules of running a sale, therefore, is understanding that misery sells: **the more miserable your customers think you are, the more they will come running**. Why? Because customers sense that if a store is in trouble and really needs money, it will have a greater tendency of reducing prices in order to generate business. In the customer's mind, the store is desperate: it just needs to turn the inventory into cash, regardless of what the merchandise cost to buy.

Customers respond to the Misery Meter subconsciously: they will flock to your sales in volumes directly proportional to their sense that your business is hurting.

The Misery Meter registers the level of misery perceived in the mind of the customer. On one end of the Misery Meter is the soft sale – the 5% off sale. Customers will come to this sale, but generally it doesn't bring out the masses. In today's

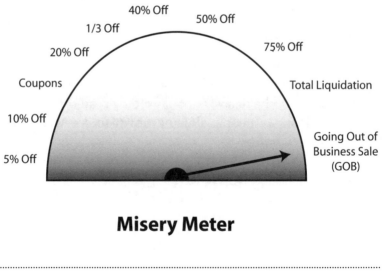

Misery Meter

competitive climate, customers look at 5% off or even 10% off as no big deal. However, there are exceptions. If a store never promotes and an item is rarely discounted, then 5% or 10% off can have a strong impact, especially if the store has a strong customer following and the % off is offered for a specified period of time. A small % off discount can motivate customers, who normally would have shopped at a store anyway, to come there during a specified time period. It's recommended that you offer a 5-10% off discount across the board on all your merchandise to get the greatest impact from this type of soft sale.

On the other end of the Misery Meter is the mega sale – the Going Out of Business Sale. This is the big one, the mother load. It's typically the once-in-a lifetime opportunity that will bring everyone out of their holes for a feeding frenzy.

The Sale Terms section contains two columns, Misery Meter and Sale Term.

Misery Meter ratings are: 1 – No Misery, 2 – Low/Medium Misery, 3 – High Misery, 4 – Unbearable Misery. This rating, when combined with the associated Sale Term enables you to convey how deep your discounts are and how desperate you are to make a sale. Make sure you don't misrepresent your pain – since that can lose you more customers in the long run.

Names can (and do) appear more than once, since the same name can be taken differently depending on context. For instance, "Gone Before You Know It" could refer to a going out of business sale (rated a 4) or to the duration of the actual sale event (rated a 2).

Remember: Don't be tied down to just the ideas here. If something gets you thinking – like the double meaning of "Pants Half Off." Think of a term that delivers a strong price message and also has a fun or playful visual. The goal is to combine laugh & learn to deliver a powerful punch and punch line. I've provided a huge list to choose from, but again use this as a jumping off point for your own creativity. Don't feel locked in just because these terms are accepted and proven. The world of retail is and will always be fueled by the different, unique, and unusual. Many of these terms were out growths or inspired by other terms. Just cause everyone uses a term is NO reason to use it but it could be.

The other side of the argument is if it's too cute it might not work. My rule on Sale and Promotional terms is the same rule I apply to a joke; if you have to explain it don't use it. But don't stop trying.

Sale Names by Misery Meter Ranking

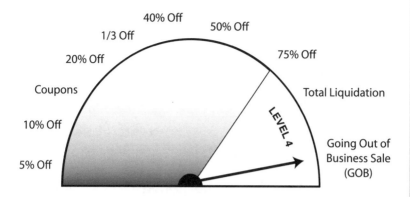

Misery Meter

LEVEL 4			
Sales Term	**Misery Meter**	**Sales Term**	**Misery Meter**
❏ 80 Percent Off	4	❏ Forced to _____	4
❏ 85 Percent Off	4	❏ Forced Liquidations	4
❏ 90 Percent Off	4	❏ Chapter 11	4
❏ 95 Percent Off	4	❏ Losing Our License	4
❏ Closing Up Shop	4	❏ Closing Forever	4
❏ Down to the Studs	4	❏ Emergency_____	4
❏ Even the Fixtures Go	4	❏ Sale Down Days	4
❏ Going Out of Business (This tells the world you are really closing)	4	❏ Sell It Down to the Drywall	4
		❏ Cash Raising	4
		❏ Need Cash	4
❏ Fixtures for Sale	4	❏ Closing Our Doors	4

Sales Term	Misery Meter	Sales Term	Misery Meter
❑ Lost Our Lease	4	❑ Moving	4
❑ Closing the Doors	4	❑ Disaster	4
❑ Lost Our License	4	❑ Everything's a Dollar	4
❑ Closing for the Season	4	❑ Fire	4
❑ Dodge the Collection Agency	4	❑ Flood	4
❑ Going Out of Retail	4	❑ Is Free Low Enough?	4
❑ Guaranteed Lowest Prices of the Year	4	❑ Let's End With a Blast	4
❑ Keep It From the Collection Agency	4	❑ Final Weekend	4
		❑ This Is Our Final, Final, Sale	4
❑ Keep the Loan Sharks at Bay	4	❑ Final Days	4
❑ Our Doors Stay Open Til Everything's Gone	4	❑ Final Winter Blast	4
		❑ It's Gotta Go	4
❑ We Broke It, You Buy It for Less	4	❑ Lunch Is On Us	4
		❑ We're Splitsville	4
❑ Gone Before You Know It	4	❑ We're Goners	4
❑ Hurricane Emergency Stock	4	❑ Lock, Stock, & Barrel	4
❑ Leaving Town	4	❑ Terrible Tuesday	4
❑ We Gotta Sell It All	4	❑ Wall to Wall	4
❑ We Missed Our Quota	4	❑ Wave the White Flag	4
❑ Let's Make the Last Sale the Best	4	❑ We Give Up	4

Sales Term	Misery Meter	Sales Term	Misery Meter
❑ We Walk a Fine Line	4	❑ Help Us Pay Our Rent	4
❑ Weak-Knee Weekend	4	❑ Creditors Are After Us Sale	4
❑ We're Outta There	4	❑ Deep in Debt Sale	4
❑ Foreclosure	4	❑ Desperate Sale	4
❑ Forced Liquidation	4	❑ Emergency Sell-Off Sale	4
❑ Court Ordered Liquidation	4	❑ Everything Must Go Sale	4
❑ Emergency Liquidation	4	❑ Fond Farewell Sale	4
❑ Emergency Sell Off	4	❑ God Help Us Sale	4
❑ Distress	4	❑ Knockin' Down the Door	4
❑ Total Liquidation	4	❑ Last Blast Sale	4
❑ Complete Liquidation	4	❑ Last Week Sale	4
❑ Final Liquidation	4	❑ Saving the Best for Last	4
❑ Final Price Reductions Taken Sale	4	❑ Under the Wire Last Sale	4

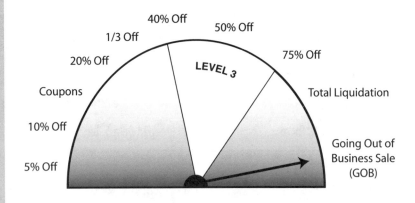

Misery Meter

LEVEL 3			
Sales Term	**Misery Meter**	**Sales Term**	**Misery Meter**
❏ Stagnant Stock	3	❏ 60 Percent Off	3
❏ 75 Percent Off	3	❏ Our Last Yearly	3
❏ 70 Percent Off	3	❏ Staff Only	3
❏ Half of Half	3	❏ Day Old for a Dollar	3
❏ Closing for the Season	3	❏ Buy One Get Two Free	3
❏ Please Buy It	3	❏ Completely Unauthorized	3
❏ One Day Only	3	❏ 50 Percent Off	3
❏ 12 Hour Marathon	3	❏ 55 Percent Off	3
❏ Expiration Day	3	❏ Biggest. Sale. Ever.	3
❏ Going, Going, Gone	3	❏ Color Mismatch	3
❏ 65 Percent Off	3	❏ Distress	3

Sales Term	Misery Meter	Sales Term	Misery Meter
❑ End of Model Year	3	❑ Double 'Em? We'll Triple Your Coupons	3
❑ Invitation Only	3	❑ Double the Rebates	3
❑ Last Chance	3	❑ End of Season	3
❑ Last Chance to Save	3	❑ Flood	3
❑ Manufacturer's Seconds	3	❑ It's the Biggest Sale of the Season	3
❑ Mismatch	3		
❑ Nearing Expiration Sale	3	❑ Keep the Man Off Our Backs	3
❑ Overstock	3		
❑ Returns & Refurbs	3	❑ Our Pain Is Your Gain	3
❑ Three for One Thursday	3	❑ Our Surplus Is Your Plus	3
❑ Basement Clear Out	3	❑ Overflowing Into the Street	3
❑ BOGO	3	❑ Pricing Gun Malfunction	3
❑ Buy One Get a Pair Free	3	❑ Scratch and Dent	3
❑ Buy One Get One Free	3	❑ So Cheap We Can't Tell HQ	3
❑ Buy the Left, Get the Right for Free	3	❑ Special Invitation Only	3
		❑ 24 Hours of Discounts	3
❑ Buy Three Get Half Off	3	❑ 99 Cents	3
❑ Buy Two Get Two Free	3	❑ All Offers Considered	3
❑ Buy Yours Get Your Friend's Free	3	❑ All Profits to Charity	3
		❑ Back Room Bargain	3
❑ Christmas Close-Out	3	❑ Bargain Basement	3

Sales Term	Misery Meter	Sales Term	Misery Meter
❑ Best Price in Town	3	❑ Ignore the Tags	3
❑ Better Than Last Year's Best	3	❑ It Might Be Free	3
❑ Bigger Than Last Year's Biggest	3	❑ Last Sale of the Summer	3
❑ Clean Us Out	3	❑ Let's Set a World Record	3
❑ Clearing Out the Cellar	3	❑ Lowest Sale	3
❑ Construction Days	3	❑ Make Room for New Stock	3
❑ Don't Make Us Move It	3	❑ Make Room for Next Year	3
❑ Don't Make Us Send It Back	3	❑ Name Your Price	3
❑ Don't Tell HQ	3	❑ On the Edge of Insanity	3
❑ Everything Below Cost	3	❑ Oops! They Goofed	3
❑ Excess Inventory	3	❑ Our Store's Anniversary	3
❑ Fall Price Freefall	3	❑ Overflow	3
❑ Gotta Get Rid of It	3	❑ Overspill Overkill	3
❑ Gotta Sell It All	3	❑ Packaging Change Over	3
❑ Hail Sale Alert	3	❑ Parking Lot	3
❑ Hailstorm	3	❑ Real Name Brands at Knockoff Prices	3
❑ Help Us Meet Quota	3	❑ Selling at a Loss	3
❑ Help Us Win Retailer of the Year	3	❑ Sidewalk	3
		❑ Slightly Irregular	3

Sales Term	Misery Meter	Sales Term	Misery Meter
❏ Slow Moving Stock	3	❏ Books by the Pound	3
❏ So Low We Can't Advertise	3	❏ Bottom Feeders	3
❏ Store Alumnus Day	3	❏ Buy Before It Expires	3
❏ Taking on the Manufacturers	3	❏ Deal of the Century	3
❏ We Bought Too Much	3	❏ Early Bird	3
❏ We Didn't Get Approval So You Save Even More	3	❏ Empty Our Coffers	3
		❏ Labor Day Truckload	3
❏ We Have No Shame	3	❏ Midnight Madness	3
❏ We Need the Space	3	❏ Our Tent Sale Is the Greatest Sale on Earth	3
❏ We Ordered Too Much	3		
❏ We're Moving	3	❏ Our Titanic Prices Sink More Each Hour	3
❏ We've Seen Better Days	3		
❏ All You Can Carry	3	❏ Over Stacked, Overstocked	3
❏ And Baby Makes 3 for 1	3	❏ Parking Lot	3
❏ Anniversary	3	❏ Penny Sale	3
❏ Annual	3	❏ Pre-Moving	3
❏ Apologies for the Construction	3	❏ Tent	3
		❏ This Is a No-Hype, No-Gimmick Sale	3
❏ Around the Clock	3		
❏ Back Alley	3	❏ Too Low to Advertise	3
❏ Big Top	3	❏ Too Low to Print	3
		❏ Top Seller Discount	3

Sales Term	Misery Meter	Sales Term	Misery Meter
❏ We're Feeling the Pinch	3	❏ End of Season Liquidation	3
❏ Prices So Low You'll Have to Duck	3	❏ Bargain Hunter's Paradise Sale	3
❏ Our Prices Were Too High	3	❏ Gotta Pay the Bills Sale	3
❏ That's Gotta Hurt	3	❏ Afraid of Our Own Prices Sale	3
❏ The Bargaining's Done – You Just Save	3	❏ Trifecta Sale – Buy 3, Get 1	3
❏ The Big Bargain Hunt	3	❏ Bargain Bonanza Sale	3
❏ The Biggest Event of the Season	3	❏ Big Mistake	3
❏ The Biggest Sale of the Season	3	❏ All Time Low Savings	3
❏ The Shirt Off Our Backs	3	❏ Amazing Savings Sale	3
❏ Why Settle for Mediocre Discounts	3	❏ Can't Believe These Prices Sale	3
❏ Yeah, It's That Good	3	❏ Defect Sale	3
❏ Double Discount Days	3	❏ Everything Out the Window	3
❏ Clearance Madness	3	❏ Final Mark Down Sale	3
❏ End of Summer Clearance	3	❏ Final Offer Sale	3
❏ Spring Remodeling Clearance	3	❏ Final Savings Sale	3
❏ Spring Fever Clearance	3	❏ Historic Savings Sale	3
❏ Cash Raising Sale	3	❏ In The Red Sale	3

Sales Term	Misery Meter	Sales Term	Misery Meter
❏ Mark Down Madness Sale	3	❏ Practically for Nothing Sale	3
❏ Mark Down Mania Sale	3	❏ Pre-Moving Sale	3
❏ Mass Sell Off Sale	3	❏ Putting Us Out of Business Sale	3
❏ Must Sell Today Sale	3	❏ Priced for Paupers Sale	3
❏ Name Your Price Sale	3	❏ Profit From Our Misery Sale	3
❏ No Price Too Low Sale	3		
❏ Overstacked & Overstocked Sale	3	❏ Shoot Ourselves in the Foot	3
❏ Rolling Back the Prices Sale	3	❏ Take It All Sale	3

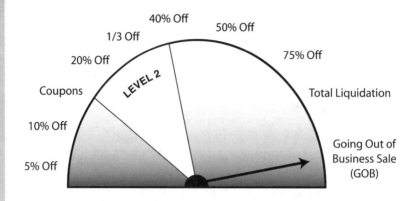

Misery Meter

LEVEL 2			
Sales Term	**Misery Meter**	**Sales Term**	**Misery Meter**
❏ Expiration Day	2	❏ Let's Make the Last Sale the Best	2
❏ Day Old Discount	2	❏ Out of Season Sale	2
❏ Gone Before You Know It	2	❏ 25 Percent Off	2
❏ Hurricane Emergency Stock	2	❏ 30 Percent Off	2
❏ We Gotta Sell It All	2	❏ 35 Percent Off	2
❏ Cheaper Than Online	2	❏ 40 Percent Off	2
❏ End of Model Year	2	❏ All Proceeds to Charity	2
❏ Exclusive Access	2	❏ All You Can Eat	2
❏ Floor Sample	2	❏ As Is	2
❏ Invite Only	2	❏ Bargain Bin	2

Sales Term	Misery Meter	Sales Term	Misery Meter
❑ Bargain Blowout	2	❑ 20 Percent Off	2
❑ Bargain Hunters	2	❑ 24 Hours of Discounts	2
❑ Biggest Sale Ever	2	❑ 99 Cents	2
❑ Buy One, Get the Second for Free	2	❑ Back Room	2
❑ Buy Three, Get Two Free	2	❑ Backroom – Wink and Save	2
❑ Buy Two, Get One Free	2	❑ Big Labor Day Weekend Storewide Sale	2
❑ Charitable	2	❑ Blue Light	2
❑ Don't Pay Til Next Year	2	❑ Bottom Dollar	2
❑ Don't Tell the Factory	2	❑ Buy 2 Get 3rd Free	2
❑ Everything's a Dollar	2	❑ Buy a Pound and Extra Ounces Are Free	2
❑ Fire	2	❑ Buy One Get the Rest for Less	2
❑ Gotta Make Room	2	❑ Buy One Get the Second Half Off	2
❑ Half Yearly	2	❑ Buy the Stereo Get the Speakers Free	2
❑ Marker Markdown	2	❑ Buy the Woofer Get the Tweeter Free	2
❑ Mooving the Herd Across Town	2	❑ Buy Three Get One Free	2
❑ One for the History Books	2	❑ Buy Two Get Half Off the Third	2
❑ Out With the Old	2		
❑ Repeat Customers Only	2		
❑ "What's Your 20" Percent Off CB Equipment	2		

2

Sales Term	Misery Meter	Sales Term	Misery Meter
❏ Dash for Savings	2	❏ Season Ending Blowout!	2
❏ Days After Christmas	2	❏ Special Discount	2
❏ Dizzy Dozen "We Only See Ten!"	2	❏ This Is Our Final, Final, Final Sale	2
❏ Double Coupon	2	❏ Who Authorized This Sale?	2
❏ Double the Difference	2		
❏ Final Weekend	2	❏ 10 Percent Off	2
❏ Four for Three Friday	2	❏ 80's Pricing Days	2
❏ Friends of the Store Only	2	❏ 90's Pricing Days	2
❏ Hats (Half) Off to You	2	❏ A Good Sale Is Hard to Find	2
❏ New Management	2		
❏ New Owner	2	❏ A Once a Year	2
❏ No Middleman	2	❏ A One-Two Punch	2
❏ No Tax	2	❏ A Person Is Known By the Discounts They Get	2
❏ Our Loss Is Your Gain	2		
❏ Out With the Old Packaging	2	❏ A Sale Four Years In the Making	2
❏ Private Back Door	2	❏ A Sale Worth Celebrating	2
❏ Rack Clearing	2	❏ A Very Merry After-Christmas Sale	2
❏ Rebate Pass-Through	2		
❏ Refer a Friend & Yours Is Free	2	❏ A Very Special Sale	2
		❏ Absence of Reason	2

Sales Term	Misery Meter	Sales Term	Misery Meter
❏ Add the Extras for Free	2	❏ Buy a Dozen & Get the Baker Free	2
❏ After Midnight	2	❏ Buy Four Get One Free	2
❏ All Things Must Pass, So Get Here Fast	2	❏ Buy One There, Get One Here	2
❏ All You Can Carry	2	❏ Buy the Pepper, Get the Salt for Free	2
❏ Amazing Savings	2	❏ Buy Two, Get Embroidery Free	2
❏ An Old-Fashioned Summertime One Cent Sale	2	❏ Buy Yours, Get Theirs Free	2
❏ Annual Tithing	2	❏ Buyer's Club Kickoff	2
❏ Another Day, Another Dollar Off	2	❏ Camp Out for Clearance	2
❏ Back to School	2	❏ Category Upgrade	2
❏ Backroom	2	❏ Caution! Deep Discounts Ahead	2
❏ Baker's Dozen	2	❏ Charity Begins With This Sale	2
❏ Be Gentle With Us	2		
❏ Be the Boss for a Day	2	❏ Christmas in July	2
❏ Beggars Can Be Choosers	2	❏ Clean Slate	2
❏ Birthday	2	❏ Client Appreciation	2
❏ Blue Ribbon	2	❏ Coming to Our Senses	2
❏ Blue Tag	2	❏ Community Appreciation	2
❏ Bring a Friend & Save More	2		

2

Sales Term	Misery Meter	Sales Term	Misery Meter
❏ Competitor Coupons	2	❏ Don't Ask, Don't Tell About Our Low Prices	2
❏ Customer Appreciation	2	❏ Don't Tell the Boss	2
❏ Customer Cash Back	2	❏ Don't Blame Us if You Miss It	2
❏ Customer Loyalty	2		
❏ Dangerously Unstable Prices	2	❏ Dream Discounts	2
❏ Deal of the Century	2	❏ Drive Your Hardest Bargain	2
❏ Design for a Dime	2	❏ Dynamite Winter Clearance	2
❏ Dig Our Discounts	2	❏ Early Bird	2
❏ Did You Hear a Manufacturer's Suggested Price?	2	❏ Everyone Gets Something Free	2
❏ Dig Up a Doozy	2	❏ Everything Below Sticker Price	2
❏ Dig Up Deals	2	❏ Factory Authorized	2
❏ Discount Awareness	2	❏ Fall in Love With Freebies	2
❏ Do It Yourself	2	❏ Fall Kickoff	2
❏ Dollar	2	❏ Final Days	2
❏ Dollar Day	2	❏ Final Winter Blast	2
❏ Dollar Off Touchdowns	2	❏ Finance It for Free	2
❏ Done and Done-er - End of Year	2	❏ Fourth & Long Bargains	2
❏ Don't Ask Why, Just Get Here	2	❏ Free Bonus	2
		❏ Free From Taxes Friday	2

Sales Term	Misery Meter	Sales Term	Misery Meter
❏ Free Gift Friday	2	❏ Hottest Sale of the Summer	2
❏ Freebie Friday	2	❏ Hurry…Before This Sale Is History	2
❏ Freedom From Finance Charges	2	❏ If We've Got It, It's on Sale	2
❏ Freedom From Oppressive Prices	2	❏ In Honor Of	2
❏ Friends & Relatives	2	❏ Is It Discounted? Count on It!	2
❏ Full Crate Discounts	2	❏ It Could Be Free Discount	2
❏ GIS Spend Fewer Bills	2	❏ It's Gotta Go	2
❏ Get Even for an Odd Price – Four for the Price of Three	2	❏ It's Not a Typo	2
❏ Get Here Early	2	❏ It's Okay to Gawk	2
❏ Get the Inspection Free	2	❏ It's OK to Leave Work Early	2
❏ Give Us Your Old One & Get Half Off	2	❏ It's Our Big Labor Day Sale	2
❏ Going Into Business Sale	2	❏ It's Our Birthday	2
❏ Grand Opening	2	❏ It's Your Birthday	2
❏ He Who Hesitates Is Missing Bargains	2	❏ It's Your Rainy Day	2
❏ Highest Quality, Cheapest Prices	2	❏ Last Week of Summer	2
❏ Holiday Coupon	2	❏ Least in the East	2
		❏ Let Us Say Thanks	2
		❏ Local Business Appreciation	2

2

Sales Term	Misery Meter	Sales Term	Misery Meter
❏ Lock in Your Prices	2	❏ Noon to Night	2
❏ Lot Clearing	2	❏ Odd Size	2
❏ Lunch Is on Us	2	❏ Once a Year	2
❏ Make a Deal	2	❏ Open Early	2
❏ Make Out Like a Bandit	2	❏ Our Annual Thanksgiving	2
❏ Make Us a Deal	2	❏ Our Annual Winter Sales Event	2
❏ Make Us an Offer	2	❏ Our Prices Have Bitten the Dust	2
❏ Midnight Madness	2		
❏ Making Room for What's Next	2	❏ Our Tent Is Still Up & Our Sale Is Still On!	2
❏ Midway Madness	2	❏ Pardon Our Construction	2
❏ Military Service Appreciation	2	❏ Our Very Merry After Christmas	2
❏ Money Multiplier	2	❏ Our Way of Saying Thanks	2
❏ More for Your Money Monday	2	❏ Pay for a Queen & Get the King	2
❏ More Than Your Money's Worth	2	❏ Pay This Time & Next Time, We'll Get It	2
❏ My How the Prices Have Fallen!	2	❏ Penny Sale	2
❏ Name Brands for Less	2	❏ Pick Your Discount	2
❏ No Questions Asked	2	❏ Pick the Score & the Item Is Free	2

Sales Term	Misery Meter	Sales Term	Misery Meter
❏ Play the Odds & Win	2	❏ Shop Til You Drop Sale	2
❏ Post Thanksgiving Warm Up	2	❏ Show Us Your Pink Slip	2
❏ President's Day Storewide	2	❏ Show Your School ID & Save	2
❏ Price Match	2		
❏ Price Slashing Winterlude	2	❏ Silver Anniversary	2
❏ Rebates Galore	2	❏ Slightly Used	2
❏ Red Tag	2	❏ So Cheap It's Free-ish	2
❏ Redecoration Days	2	❏ So Exclusive We Almost Couldn't Get In!	2
❏ Retail Price, Shmeetail Price	2		
		❏ So Low It's Gonna Hurt	2
❏ Repeat Customer Appreciation	2	❏ So Many Choices	2
		❏ Spillover	2
❏ Roll the Dice & Save	2	❏ Some Are Born Discounted, Some Achieve Discounts, & Some Have Discounts Thrust Upon Them	2
❏ Rotating Stock	2		
❏ Round Down	2		
❏ Satisfaction Guaranteed Saturday	2		
		❏ Spin the Wheel	2
❏ Save as Much as You Want	2	❏ Spring Tent	2
❏ Secret Coupon Sale	2	❏ Stick Us With the Sales Tax	2
❏ Secret Deals	2	❏ Stick Us With the Shipping	2
❏ Secret Santa Deals	2	❏ Stock Moving	2
❏ Select Your Price Saturday	2	❏ Store Redesign	2

2

Sales Term	Misery Meter	Sales Term	Misery Meter
❏ Storewide Anniversary	2	❏ This Year's Fashions, Last Year's Prices	2
❏ Suggested Prices Are for Losers	2	❏ Tie One on, Get One in the Bag for Free	2
❏ Such a Deal	2	❏ Time Is Running Out Sale	2
❏ Tax Free	2	❏ Top Secret	2
❏ Tax Freedom	2	❏ Trade In	2
❏ Tear Down This Wall (We Need the Room!)	2	❏ Trade It In	2
❏ Thanks for Coming Back	2	❏ Truckload	2
❏ Thanks for Being Part of the Family	2	❏ 2 for 1 Tuesday	2
❏ Thanks for the Loyalty	2	❏ Under New Management	2
❏ Thanks for Stickin' With Us	2	❏ Valued Customers Only	2
❏ They Won't Take It Back	2	❏ Veterans' Day	2
❏ There's No Free Lunch (Except Today!)	2	❏ Veterans' Day Weekend	2
❏ They Said We Couldn't Do It	2	❏ Wave Goodbye to List Prices	2
❏ Too Much Stuff	2	❏ We Get It for Less	2
❏ This Qualifies as a Family Emergency	2	❏ We Bargained – You Don't Have To	2
❏ This Sale Is So Good We're Throwing a Party	2	❏ We Got It Lower	2
		❏ We Didn't Change a Thing…Except the Prices!	2

Sales Term	Misery Meter	Sales Term	Misery Meter
❏ We Got Your Tax	2	❏ We're Still Here	2
❏ We Saved the Best Sale for Last	2	❏ We're Throwing in the Free Stuff	2
❏ We Gotta Pay Vito	2	❏ We've Got It All Discounted	2
❏ Welcome Back	2	❏ We're Overstocked, So We're Underselling	2
❏ Well Below Market Value	2		
❏ Well Below Retail	2	❏ We've Passed the Savings on to You	2
❏ We'll Double Your Warranty	2	❏ What Will You Do With the Extra Money?	2
❏ We'll Get the Tax	2		
❏ We'll Match Any Price	2	❏ When We Get a Price Break, You Get a _____	2
❏ We'll Pay the Pennies	2		
❏ We'll Pay You to Pick It Up	2	❏ Who Needs Christmas Wrap in January?	2
❏ We'll-Pay-the-Tax	2	❏ Will the Discounts Ever End	2
❏ We're Back Again!	2	❏ Winter Products at Summer Prices	2
❏ We're Expanding	2		
❏ We're Goners	2	❏ Winter's Splintered & Dented	2
❏ We're Gonna Say Yes	2		
❏ We're Hurting Here	2	❏ Winvitation Only	2
❏ We're Passing on Profits	2	❏ Yard	2
❏ We're Ready to Deal	2	❏ Yellow Tag	2
❏ We're Splitsville	2	❏ Yes Folks It Has Frozen Over	2

Sales Term	Misery Meter	Sales Term	Misery Meter
❏ You Don't Have to Tell Them It Was on Sale	2	❏ Buy Now, Pay Later	2
❏ You're the Boss	2	❏ Buy One & We'll Throw in the Towel	2
❏ Zip Up a Package Deal	2	❏ Can the Costs	2
❏ A Day Late & a Dollar Less	2	❏ Circus Tent	2
❏ A Spring Sale So Hot, You'll Think It's Summer	2	❏ Dark Alley	2
❏ A Summer Sale So Big They'll Be Saving in Places Where It Isn't Even Summer	2	❏ Don't Let This Sale Away	2
		❏ Even Hour Deals	2
❏ All Is Not Lost, But It's Less	2	❏ Everything Turkey Related for Less	2
❏ All the Best for Less	2	❏ Freaky Friday	2
❏ All's Cheap That Ends Cheap	2	❏ Get While the Getting's Good	2
❏ Amazing Summer's End	2	❏ Gigantic January	2
❏ Bangle Bargain Days	2	❏ Grab It And Run	2
❏ Best in the West	2	❏ Great Deals – No Waiting	2
❏ Best of All Worlds	2	❏ Hourly Special	2
❏ Best of Fall	2	❏ How Do You Like Us Now	2
❏ Best of the Best	2	❏ How Else Can We Say Thanks?	2
❏ Best Sellers for Less	2	❏ Ice Cream for Everybody	2
❏ Burst Our Bubble	2	❏ If It's Made Here the Deals Are Clear	2

Sales Term	Misery Meter	Sales Term	Misery Meter
❏ If It's Sweet, It's on Sale	2	❏ Our Deals Are Smokin'	2
❏ If You Snooze You Lose	2	❏ Our Discounts Are Automatic	2
❏ It Was State of the Art at Some Point	2	❏ Our Doors Are Still Open	2
❏ It's About Value	2	❏ Our Discounts Will Sleigh You	2
❏ It's Real, We Promise!	2	❏ Our Needle Is on Savings	2
❏ Kick Off the Season	2	❏ Our Sale Prices Beat Their Sale Prices	2
❏ Last Month's Fad	2	❏ Pants Half Off	2
❏ Leave With More Bills	2	❏ Prices Are Falling	2
❏ Lock Down a Deal	2	❏ Prices Are Falling With the Leaves	2
❏ Luxury for Less	2	❏ Prices Are Melting During Our Spring Thaw Sale	2
❏ Make It a Double	2	❏ Prices Lower Than the Titanic	2
❏ Merchandise Mix-Up	2	❏ Prices as Loose as an Unstuck Wicket	2
❏ Not for the Timid	2		
❏ Not for the Faint of Heart	2	❏ Print It at Home, Save Here	2
❏ Not What's Expected	2	❏ Push Our Buttons & Save	2
❏ Not Your Average	2	❏ Put Us Through the Wringer	2
❏ Now This Is an Exclusive	2		
❏ October Thank You Days	2		
❏ One Hail of A	2		
❏ Oops We Did It Again	2		

Sales Term	Misery Meter	Sales Term	Misery Meter
❏ Random Rack	2	❏ Stop the Madness	2
❏ Read Into Rebates	2	❏ Surprise Discount	2
❏ Reap Our Discounts	2	❏ Tag	2
❏ Say What?!	2	❏ Take a Tax Holiday	2
❏ Sale? You Can't Handle This Sale	2	❏ Tell Us Where to Stick It	2
❏ Sew Up Your Bargains	2	❏ The Bargains Only Come Out at Night	2
❏ Score One for the Little Guys	2	❏ The Getting Is Good	2
❏ Shame on Us	2	❏ The Gold Rush	2
❏ Signs Point to Discounts	2	❏ The Mice Will Play	2
❏ Sink Into Savings	2	❏ The Most Bone Chilling Sale Ever	2
❏ Spring (Price) Break	2	❏ The Rainy Day Sale Is Here	2
❏ Spring Gala	2	❏ The Presidents' Day Sale That Gives You Something to Celebrate	2
❏ Spring Jubilee	2	❏ The Road to Savings Is Paved With Our Coupons	2
❏ Spring Pilgrimage	2		
❏ Spring Price Buster	2		
❏ Spring Spectacular	2	❏ The Sale Justifies the Means	2
❏ Stick It to Us	2		
❏ Stick to Your Guns	2	❏ The Season Is the Reason	2
❏ Stick Us With the Bill	2	❏ The Sale You've Been Waiting For	2

Sales Term	Misery Meter	Sales Term	Misery Meter
❏ Their Loss Is Your Gain	2	❏ We're Off Our Game	2
❏ Throw the Dart	2	❏ We're Out of Our Minds	2
❏ Throwback Pricing	2	❏ We're Talking Bargains	2
❏ Tip of the Iceberg	2	❏ We've Flipped Our Lid	2
❏ Truck	2	❏ We've Got It Right This Time	2
❏ Wall to Wall	2	❏ We've Lowered Prices– Again!	2
❏ Wanted: Our Regular Customers	2	❏ We've Renewed the Lease	2
❏ Warm Up to Our Winter Bargains	2	❏ What Gives You the Right to Save So Much?	2
❏ Wave the White Flag	2	❏ What's It Gonna Take	2
❏ We Can't Be Serious, But We Are!	2	❏ Where Else Are You Gonna Save So Much?	2
❏ We Give Up!	2	❏ Winter Carnival	2
❏ We Love Our Customers	2	❏ Winter Luau	2
❏ We Walk a Fine Line	2	❏ Winter Madness	2
❏ Weak-Knee Weekend	2	❏ Write Your Own Coupon	2
❏ We'll Show You the Love	2	❏ You Asked for It	2
❏ We'll Show You the Money (Back)	2	❏ You Asked for It, You Got It	2
❏ We're a Little Loopy	2	❏ You Bring the Wheels & We'll Bring the Deals	2
❏ We're in Your Corner	2		

2

Sales Term	Misery Meter	Sales Term	Misery Meter
❑ You Can Have It for Less	2	❑ Senior Citizens' Cash	2
❑ You Can Have It All	2	❑ Discount Coupon	2
❑ You Can't Beat the Deals	2	❑ Hats Off to Savings Sale	2
❑ You Can't Fight It Any Longer	2	❑ Blizzard Blowout Sale	2
❑ You Can't Get It for Less	2	❑ Hotel Sale	2
❑ You Deserve It	2	❑ Store Wide Sale	2
❑ You Don't Even Have to Ask	2	❑ An Irresistible Sale	2
❑ You Need to See This	2	❑ A Special Sale	2
❑ You Want It, You Got It!	2	❑ Back to Reality	2
❑ You'll Be Shocked By the Savings	2	❑ Bank on Saving	2
❑ You'll Be Taken Back by Our Savings	2	❑ Best Buys in Town Sale	2
❑ You'll Remember This Presidents' Day	2	❑ Bonus Days	2
❑ You'll Thank Us for Telling You About It	2	❑ Breaking Records Sale	2
❑ Your Discount Is in the Cards	2	❑ Bulls-Eye Savings	2
❑ Your Doctor Can Write You a Note…Because He'll Be Here Too!	2	❑ Budget Breakers Sale	2
		❑ Buying Bonanza Sale	2
		❑ Fat Savings Sale	2
		❑ Daily Knockdown Sale	2
		❑ Dirt Cheap Prices Sale	2
		❑ Dollar Mania Sale	2
		❑ Door Buster Sale	2
		❑ Dynamite Day Sale	2

Sales Term	Misery Meter	Sales Term	Misery Meter
❏ God Help Us Sale	2	❏ Monster Sale	2
❏ Knocking Down the Door	2	❏ Monster Mash Sale Bash	2
❏ Good News for Your Pocketbook	2	❏ Mop Up the Savings	2
		❏ New Start Sale	2
❏ Last Blast Sale	2	❏ Night Sale	2
❏ Last Minute Sale	2	❏ Kick Off the Season Sale	2
❏ Gotta Stock Up Sale	2	❏ Killer Prices Sale	2
❏ Half Yearly Sale	2	❏ No Limit Sale	2
❏ Hang Onto Your Money Sale	2	❏ No Hype No Gimmicks Sale	2
❏ Holiday Hangover Sale	2	❏ Off Our Rocker Sale	2
❏ Holiday Wrap Up Sale	2	❏ Old Fashioned Savings Sale	2
❏ How Low Can We Go Sale	2		
❏ Instant Sale	2	❏ Only the Best Prices Sale	2
❏ Instant Savings Sale	2	❏ Please Buy It Sale	2
❏ Irresistible Sale	2	❏ Preferred Customer Sale	2
❏ Locals Special Sale	2	❏ Product of the Week	2
❏ Loyal Customer Sale	2	❏ Punch on the Stomach Sale	2
❏ Making Space Sale	2		
❏ Manager's Special Sale	2	❏ Really Big Sale	2
❏ Marathon Sale	2	❏ Road Map to Savings	2
❏ Members Only Sale	2	❏ Rock Bottom Sale	2

2

Sales Term	Misery Meter	Sales Term	Misery Meter
❏ Save a Buck Sale	2	❏ Something for Nothing Sale	2
❏ Save a Bundle Sale	2	❏ Smart Shopper Sale	2
❏ Save a Wad This Weekend	2	❏ The Next Season Sale	2
❏ Save Now and Later Sale	2	❏ Take It All Sale	2
❏ Saving the Best for Last Sale	2	❏ Tap Into Big Savings Sale	2
❏ Say Hello to Good Buys	2	❏ Trade in Sale	2
❏ Score Big Sale	2	❏ Twas the Sale Before Christmas	2
❏ Secret Savings Sale	2	❏ Unbelievable Prices Sale	2
❏ Price Crusher	2	❏ Under the Wire Last Sale	2
❏ Priced for Last Century Sale	2	❏ VIP Sale	2
❏ Priced to Go Sale	2	❏ Wait No Longer Sale	2
❏ Priced to Move Sale	2	❏ We Can't Keep It Sale	2
❏ Priced to Save Sale	2	❏ We Have No Room Sale	2
❏ Private Back Room Sale	2	❏ We Must Be Crazy Sale	2
❏ Private Back Door Sale	2	❏ We Must Be Drunk Sale	2
❏ Rock Bottom Savings	2	❏ Wheeling and Dealing Sale	2
❏ Seeing Is Believing Sale	2	❏ Yule Tide Savings Sale	2
❏ Serious Savings Sale	2	❏ Zero Mark Up Sale	2
❏ Shameless Sale	2		
❏ Shop Til You Drop Sale	2		

2

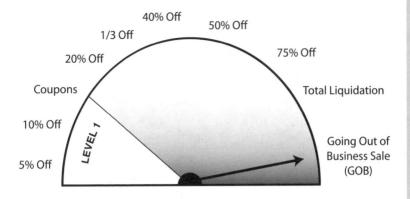

Misery Meter

LEVEL 1			
Sales Term	**Misery Meter**	**Sales Term**	**Misery Meter**
❏ Leaving Town	1	❏ 9 to 5	1
❏ Let's End With a Blast	1	❏ A Chain Is Only as Strong as Its Lowest Prices	1
❏ Sidewalk BBQ	1		
❏ Don't Forget the Discounts	1	❏ A Friend in Need Is a Friend Indeed	1
❏ End of Month	1		
❏ 12 Hour	1	❏ Bargain Safari	1
❏ 2 Day	1	❏ Buy Five Get One Free	1
❏ 24 Hour	1	❏ Buy New Shoes & Get a Free Shine	1
❏ 48 Hour	1		
❏ 72 Hour	1	❏ Buy Our Stuff Please!	1
❏ 8 Hour	1	❏ Buy the Cap, Give Us the Bill	1

Sales Term	Misery Meter	Sales Term	Misery Meter
❏ Buy the Cloth, Get Fringe Benefits	1	❏ Open Late	1
❏ December Sales if It Snows	1	❏ Our Cup Runneth Over	1
❏ Discounts Are a Dish Best Served Hot!	1	❏ Pink Slip Party	1
❏ Extended Family	1	❏ Pink Slip Sale	1
❏ Flattery Will Get You Discounts	1	❏ Pitch In and Save	1
❏ Founders Day	1	❏ Power Buying Is Key	1
❏ Fresh From the Garden	1	❏ Select	1
❏ Fresh Off the Farm	1	❏ I "Voted" for Discounts	1
❏ Gift Trade In	1	❏ "Whoa" Is You	1
❏ Guess the Score & It's Free	1	❏ A Bike Tune Up	1
❏ Happy Hour	1	❏ A Bundle of Joy	1
❏ In Remembrance	1	❏ A Concrete	1
❏ Incorporation Day	1	❏ A Discount Wrapped Up in an Enigma	1
❏ Inventory	1	❏ A Drum Sale That Can't Be Beat	1
❏ January 1 – Our Biggest Sale So Far	1	❏ A Flag Waving	1
❏ Just for the Weekend	1	❏ A Kickin' Boot Sale	1
❏ Luau in Winter	1	❏ A Little Knowledge Is a Dangerous Thing, but This Sale Isn't	1
❏ Money Tree	1	❏ A Lot of Lots	1
		❏ A Mind Expanding Back to School	1

1

Sales Term	Misery Meter	Sales Term	Misery Meter
❏ A Nine Inning	1	❏ After Father's Day	1
❏ A Pearl of a Sale	1	❏ After All, This Sale Is All Downhill	1
❏ A Penny Saved Is Not Enough	1	❏ After Thanksgiving Coupon	1
❏ A Picture's Worth at Least _____	1	❏ After Thanksgiving	1
❏ A Presidents' Day Sale You've Never Seen	1	❏ Ain't Nothing but Savings	1
❏ A Sale for Everything & Everything Is on Sale	1	❏ Aisles of Smiles	1
		❏ All American	1
❏ A Sale of a Different Color	1	❏ All Caps on Sale	1
❏ A Sale With Great Worth	1	❏ All Discounts Must Pass	1
❏ A Sale With Some Muscle Behind It	1	❏ All I Want for Christmas Is on Sale	1
❏ A Sweetheart of a	1	❏ All Merchandise Reduced	1
❏ A Woman's Place Is at Our	1	❏ All Roads Lead to This	1
❏ A Sweetheart of a Deal and a Cupid of a	1	❏ All That Glitters Is Gold	1
		❏ All That Glitters Is Not Gold (We've Got Diamonds Too!)	1
❏ A Thanksgiving Sale With All the Trimmings	1	❏ All Things to All People	1
❏ A Winter Sale You'll Warm Up To	1	❏ All You Need Is Love	1
		❏ All American Sale That's Out of the Blue	1
❏ Acres of Spring	1		
❏ Advertised	1	❏ Ambidextrous	1

Sales Term	Misery Meter	Sales Term	Misery Meter
❑ And All Through the House	1	❑ Baby Boom	1
❑ And the Kitchen Sink Too	1	❑ Baby Day	1
❑ Animal Brand	1	❑ Back 2 School	1
❑ Annual Summer Scorcher	1	❑ Back at Class… Everything's Now On	1
❑ Anti-Diet	1	❑ Back at School	1
❑ April Action	1	❑ Back Atcha	1
❑ April Showers Bring Discounts	1	❑ Back From School	1
❑ Arrive in Your Old Car, Leave in Your New One	1	❑ Back From the Front	1
❑ Arsenic Hour	1	❑ Back It Up, Load It In	1
❑ Art Appreciation	1	❑ Back to School Kick Off	1
❑ As Good as Gold	1	❑ Back to Basics	1
❑ As if We Need a Reason for a Sale	1	❑ Back to the Dorm	1
❑ As Seen on Television	1	❑ Back Up the Truck	1
❑ As Seen on TV	1	❑ Bag a Deal	1
❑ At the Head of the Class	1	❑ Banker's Hours	1
❑ Ask Not for Whom the Prices Fall. They Fall for Thee	1	❑ Be Afraid. Be Very Afraid.	1
❑ Autumn Color Accent	1	❑ Be All You Can Be	1
❑ Away Game	1	❑ Be in the Game	1
		❑ Be Prepared	1
		❑ Be the Early Bird	1

Sales Term	Misery Meter	Sales Term	Misery Meter
❏ Be the Joneses	1	❏ Big Birthday	1
❏ Be the One They Envy	1	❏ Big Game	1
❏ Be the Sale You Want to Be	1	❏ Billion Dollar	1
❏ Be Your Own Role Model	1	❏ Bird in the Hand	1
❏ Beauty Is in the Eye of the Beholder	1	❏ Birds of a Feather Flock to Our Sale	1
❏ Because We Feel Like It	1	❏ Bite Into Savings	1
❏ Because We Can	1	❏ Black Cat	1
❏ Before You Hit the Mountains, Hit Our Ski Sale	1	❏ Blazing Boot	1
		❏ Bling Bling	1
❏ Best Foot Forward	1	❏ Blood Donor Discounts	1
❏ Best Get Here Fast	1	❏ Blower Blowout	1
❏ Best of Both Worlds	1	❏ Blue & Grey	1
❏ Best of the Best	1	❏ Blue & Gold	1
❏ Best Seller Book	1	❏ Blue Moon	1
❏ Better Late Than Never	1	❏ Bold Gold	1
❏ Better Off Red	1	❏ Book	1
❏ Better on the Inside	1	❏ Book Your Own Adventure	1
❏ Better Safe Than Sorry	1	❏ Boost the Economy	1
❏ Beyond Excitement	1	❏ Boys of Summer	1
❏ Big Baby Day	1	❏ Boy's Toys	1

1

Sales Term	Misery Meter	Sales Term	Misery Meter
❏ Boys Will Be Boys	1	❏ Buy a Set and Save	1
❏ Brand Name	1	❏ Buy a Vowel	1
❏ Brand New Bag	1	❏ Buy All You Want We'll Make More	1
❏ Bread & Butter	1		
❏ Break Down the Doors	1	❏ Buy Buy Blackbird	1
❏ Break Open the Piggy Bank – You Can Afford It Now	1	❏ Buy Her Happiness	1
		❏ Buy in Bulk & Save	1
❏ Breakfast Hour	1	❏ Buy Into Health	1
❏ Breathe in the Savings	1	❏ Buy Into the Lifestyle	1
❏ Bring Down the House	1	❏ Buy It Again	1
❏ Bring It On	1	❏ Buy It Today We'll install It Tomorrow	1
❏ Bring on the Season	1		
❏ Bring Them Home	1	❏ Buy It, You'll Like It	1
❏ Bring Us Your Tired	1	❏ Buy More Time	1
❏ Bring Your Own Bag	1	❏ Buy One…That's It!	1
❏ Broaden Your Horizons	1	❏ Buy Our Stuff	1
❏ Brunch Hour	1	❏ Buy Some Time	1
❏ Build Your Dream _____	1	❏ Buy the Car & Get the Wheels Free	1
❏ Buttoned Down	1		
❏ Buy a New Coat of Paint	1	❏ Buy the Cow Cuz the Milk Ain't Free	1
		❏ Buy the Farm, and Live!	1

Sales Term	Misery Meter	Sales Term	Misery Meter
❑ Buy 2 Rabbits, Get More Free	1	❑ Cheque Us Out	1
❑ Buy Your Happiness	1	❑ Children's Hour	1
❑ Cabin Fever	1	❑ Circle the Wagons	1
❑ Call It Whatever You Want	1	❑ City Lights	1
❑ Can We Talk … About Deals?	1	❑ Clean Out Your Closet	1
❑ Can You Tell the Difference	1	❑ Clean Up on Detergents & Cleansers	1
❑ Cans for Coins	1	❑ Clean Up on Spring	1
❑ Capture the Feeling	1	❑ Clear Out the Clutter	1
❑ Capture the Moment	1	❑ Close Your Mouth	1
❑ Casino Night	1	❑ C'mon, Give Us a Try	1
❑ Catch the _____ Sale Wave	1	❑ Cocktail Hour	1
❑ Catch the Spirit	1	❑ Cogito Ergo Save	1
❑ Caught You Looking	1	❑ Columbus Day Sailing Savings	1
❑ Celebrate Summer	1	❑ Columbus Day Weekend	1
❑ Celebrate the Almighty Dollar	1	❑ Come in Out of the Cold	1
❑ Celebrity Look Alike	1	❑ Come Say Howdy	1
❑ Century	1	❑ Comfortable Living on Now	1
❑ Check the Digits	1	❑ Confusion Sale	1
		❑ Consignment	1

1

Sales Term	Misery Meter	Sales Term	Misery Meter
❏ Corner the Market on Produce	1 1	❏ Dig Our Well Equipment	1
❏ Count to Ten & Come on In	1	❏ Dinner Hour	1
❏ Country Fair	1	❏ Discounts by the Yard	1
❏ Country Jamboree	1	❏ Discover the Great Columbus Day Sale	1
❏ Crazy	1	❏ Discovery Day	1
❏ Cross Country Ski Sale	1	❏ Do Unto Others	1
❏ Cupboard Bare? Fill 'Em for Less	1	❏ Does It Ever End	1
❏ Customize Your Package	1	❏ Dog Days	1
❏ Cushion Your Fall Pillow Sale	1	❏ Doggone Great	1
		❏ Dogs Eat Free	1
❏ Dad's Day	1	❏ Don't Be Blue	1
❏ Daily Revenue Lottery	1	❏ Don't Deny Your Urges	1
❏ Decorate the Nursery	1	❏ Don't Give In to High Prices	1
❏ Declare Independence From High Prices	1	❏ Don't Just Watch It Through the Window	1
❏ Defrost February Savings	1	❏ Don't Let This Sale Make You Think You're a Sucker	1
❏ Democracy Appreciation	1	❏ Don't Miss It, or You Will Be the April Fool	1
❏ Desperate Housewives	1	❏ Don't Stop Thinking About Tomorrow	1
❏ Dieter's Dream	1		
❏ Diet-Free Zone	1	❏ Don't Tell Mom	1

Sales Term	Misery Meter	Sales Term	Misery Meter
❏ Don't Tell the Neighbors	1	❏ Economic Upturn	1
❏ Dorm Daze	1	❏ Eggcellent Easter Discounts	1
❏ Down the Chimney	1	❏ Eggstraordinarily Special Easter	1
❏ Down to the Wire	1		
❏ Downhill Ski	1	❏ Elect to Save More	1
❏ Draw a Bead on Art Deals	1	❏ Election Day Voter	1
❏ Dress for Success	1	❏ Enough Is Enough	1
❏ Dress Your Windows for Winter	1	❏ Every Day Is Thanksgiving Day	1
❏ Drill Us for Discounts on Bits	1	❏ Every Monday in May	1
❏ Drive Home Our Bargains	1	❏ Everything Black	1
❏ Drop the Remote	1	❏ Everything Blue	1
❏ Dust to Dust Housecleaning	1	❏ Everything for Your Honey on Sale	1
❏ Early Bird	1	❏ Everything Has Its (Lowered) Price	1
❏ Early to Bed	1		
❏ Early to Rise	1	❏ Everything Looks Better On	1
❏ Easter's Best	1	❏ Everything Nines	1
❏ Easy Come, Easy Go	1	❏ Everything Red	1
❏ Eat Slower & Savor the Savings	1	❏ Everything Red, White & Blue	1

Sales Term	Misery Meter	Sales Term	Misery Meter
❑ Expect the Unexpected	1	❑ Familiarity Breeds Discounts	1
❑ Fall Clean Up	1	❑ Fan Appreciation	1
❑ Fall Family Week	1	❑ FanTastic	1
❑ Fall Fashion Week	1	❑ Fast Forward to DVD Ownership	1
❑ Fall Fest	1		
❑ Fall Festival	1	❑ Feel at Home With Our Range	1
❑ Fall Festival of Leaves	1		
❑ Fall Fiesta	1	❑ Festival of Lights	1
❑ Fall Furniture Extravaganza	1	❑ Figaro's "Me, Me, Me!" Event	1
❑ Fall Home Festival	1	❑ Fill 'Er Up for Less	1
❑ Fall in Love All Over Again	1	❑ Fill the Pail	1
❑ Fall Into a Great	1	❑ Fill Your Cart & Save	1
❑ Fall Into Fashion	1	❑ Fill Your Cellar	1
❑ Fall Into Our	1	❑ Fill Your Coffers	1
❑ Fall Lawn & Garden	1	❑ Find the Time	1
❑ Fall Savings Stock Up	1	❑ Finally, a No Nonsense Straight Forward Sales Event	1
❑ Fall Starts Here… With Our Super Fall Sale	1		
❑ Fall Stock Up Selection	1	❑ Finders Keepers	1
❑ Falling Needles, Falling Prices	1	❑ Firecracker	1
		❑ First Day of Summer	1

Sales Term	Misery Meter	Sales Term	Misery Meter
❏ First Dollar Day	1	❏ For Your One in a Million Girl	1
❏ First Friday Bargains	1	❏ Fortune Cookie Freebies	1
❏ First on the Block	1	❏ Fortune's Smiling on You	1
❏ First Snow	1	❏ Four Hour	1
❏ First Things First	1	❏ Frame Your Discounts	1
❏ Fish Out Your Discounts	1	❏ Frappe Friday	1
❏ Fixin's Are Free	1	❏ Freaky Friday	1
❏ Flat Out Rugs	1	❏ Free Dog Wash With Every _____	1
❏ Flat Fee Flats	1	❏ Free Financing	1
❏ Flip a Coin	1	❏ Freedom to Save More	1
❏ Flip Our Lid	1	❏ Free-Range Naugahyde	1
❏ Flip Us for It	1	❏ Fresh Fashion	1
❏ Flippin' Bargains	1	❏ Frogs & Toads Are On	1
❏ Flu Season Deferral	1	❏ Friends, Romans, Countrymen	1
❏ Fluffy Stuff	1	❏ From Aisle to Isle	1
❏ Flying Pig	1	❏ From Sale to Shining Sale	1
❏ Focus on Saving More	1	❏ Frozen Goods Friday	1
❏ Foolishly Large	1	❏ Full Day of Discounts	1
❏ For Better or for Best	1	❏ Gab & Gossip	1
❏ For Better or for Worse	1	❏ Garage	1
❏ For the Love of All That Is Hold-y	1		

1

Sales Term	Misery Meter	Sales Term	Misery Meter
Gardening Season	1	Get Stoked at Our Wood Stove Sale	1
Gather Round the Maypole	1	Get the Goods	1
Gather Ye Roses	1	Get the Lead Out	1
Gem (and Jewel) of a Sale	1	Get the Look You Like	1
Get a Great Deal During the Real	1	Get the Low Down	1
Get All Up in Our Grills	1	What You Really Wanted	1
Get an A & Save	1	Get What You Want	1
Get Caught Up on Shopping	1	Get Your Groove On	1
Get Growing Lawn	1	Get Your Gift for Your Juliet Yet?	1
Get It All Here	1	Gimme a Back to School	1
Get It for Less	1	Give Back to the Community Day	1
Get It Out of My Store & Into Your Car	1	Give Us the Heave Ho!	1
Get It to Go	1	Give High Prices the Heave Ho!	1
Get It, Got It, Good	1	Go With Dog	1
Get Milk	1	Going Online	1
Get Outta Town	1	Golf Sale for Dad	1
Get Ready for Bikini Season	1	Good for the Soul Sunday	1
Get Santa to OK This	1	Good Night Sweetheart, It's Time to Go	1
Get Set for Spring	1		

Sales Term	Misery Meter	Sales Term	Misery Meter
❑ Good Sheets	1	❑ Hail to ____ Fantastic Money Saving Sale	1
❑ Good Things Come to Those Who Wait	1	❑ Hail to the Chief, What a Relief! It's Sale Time	1
❑ Got a Better Idea for a Sale	1	❑ Hair Today, Gone Tomorrow Wig Sale	1
❑ Gotta Get It Sale	1		
❑ Gotta Move 'Em Out	1	❑ Hang Onto Your Money, It's on Sale	1
❑ Grab a Cold One	1		
❑ Grab Your Girl and Go	1	❑ Happy Days Are Here Again	1
❑ Grab Your Guy and Go	1		
❑ Grand Slam Sunday	1	❑ Happy Easter	1
❑ Granny Hour	1	❑ Hard Bargains on Software	1
❑ Great Cheese Event	1	❑ Haste Makes Waist	1
❑ Great Goods for Grandparents	1	❑ Haste Makes Wonderful Savings	1
❑ Great Green Goods Greenback Giveback	1	❑ Haunted House	1
❑ Great Gridiron Days Grills	1	❑ Have a Little Mercy	1
❑ Great Memories for Less	1	❑ Have Your Cake	1
❑ Great Minds Shop Here	1	❑ Haven't Seen You in a While Sale	1
❑ Green Tag	1		
❑ Grow a Garden	1	❑ Heads You Win	1
❑ Guess the Discount & Win	1	❑ He Who Laughs Last Must've Been Here	1

Sales Term	Misery Meter	Sales Term	Misery Meter
❏ Hecks – We've Got All the Sinks On	1	❏ Holiday Wrap Up	1
❏ Help Us Beat Our Sales GOOOOOOOOOOOAL!	1	❏ Home Field advantage	1
❏ Help Us Out	1	❏ Home for the Holiday	1
❏ Hems Are Rising, Prices Are Falling	1	❏ Home Game	1
❏ Here Comes the Birdie	1	❏ Home Improvement	1
❏ Here Comes the Bride	1	❏ Home Is Where the Sale Is	1
❏ Here on Business	1	❏ Home Office	1
❏ Here's a Sale That's Just Ducky	1	❏ Home Office Upgrade	1
❏ Hey Come Back Here	1	❏ Honest Abe	1
❏ Hey Nice Pants!	1	❏ Honor the Great Ones	1
❏ Hide the Receipt	1	❏ Hooked on Our Fish	1
❏ High Noon Sale	1	❏ Hoops Fever	1
❏ High Steaks, Low Prices	1	❏ Hooray for Capitalism	1
❏ His & Hers	1	❏ Hot 4th of July Sale	1
❏ Hit the Beach	1	❏ Hot Deals for Cold Months	1
❏ Hoagies & Stogies	1	❏ Hourly Changeover	1
❏ Hole in the Wall	1	❏ How to Wrap Up a Sale	1
❏ Hoe Hoe Hoe! Garden Goods Here	1	❏ How Many Candles Will These Presidents Be Blowing Out During Our Blow Out?	1
		❏ Humbugs Aren't invited	1
		❏ Hunt Down Low Prices	1

Sales Term	Misery Meter	Sales Term	Misery Meter
❏ Hunting for a Great Sale?	1	❏ If You Can Say It, It's on Sale	1
❏ Hurricane Hour	1	❏ If You Can Spell It, It's on Sale	1
❏ I See London, I See France	1	❏ If You Can't Beat 'Em, Join 'Em	1
❏ I Can't Believe They Still Make These	1	❏ If You Can't Stand the Heat, C'mon in Here	1
❏ I Spy Savings	1	❏ If You Weren't Meant to Spend, Then Why Do You Have Money?	1
❏ I Spy With My Little Eye – Incredible Deals	1		
❏ Ice Cold	1	❏ If You're in You Win	1
❏ I Thought a Quarterback Was a Great Sale!	1	❏ If You've Been Here Before You'll Save	1
❏ I'd Buy That for a Dollar	1	❏ In a Blaze of Glory… Veterans' Day	1
❏ If It Doesn't Rhyme With Orange	1	❏ In & Out in an Hour	1
❏ If It Roars, It's Yours	1	❏ In the Beginning Was the Sale	1
❏ If It's in the Rainbow, It's Reduced	1	❏ Inn Conceivable Prices	1
❏ If It's Local It's Less	1	❏ Invest in Yourself	1
❏ If Not Now, Then When	1	❏ Is It Ever Enough	1
❏ If Your Name Is _____	1	❏ Is This Enough	1
❏ Imports	1	❏ Isn't This Something	1
❏ If You Can Read This You Save!	1		

Sales Term	Misery Meter	Sales Term	Misery Meter
❏ It Goes With Big Savings	1	❏ It's New to You	1
❏ It Goes Without Saying	1	❏ It's OK to Count Your Chickens	1
❏ It Is Rocket Science – Text Book Sale	1	❏ It's OK to Play	1
❏ It Takes a Sale to Catch Bargains	1	❏ It's Our First Time	1
❏ It Takes One to Know One	1	❏ It's Safe to Come Inside	1
❏ It's a Monster of a	1	❏ It's Safe to Come Outside	1
❏ It's a Walk-away	1	❏ It's the Best Back-To-School Sale in Its Class	1
❏ It's a Wrap	1	❏ It's the Easiest Sale You've Ever Seen	1
❏ It's an Irresistible	1	❏ It's the One You've Been Waiting For	1
❏ It's Better Than a	1	❏ It's Tick Season, Do You Have Your Clock?	1
❏ It's Better to Give, So Let Us!	1	❏ It's Useless to Resist It	1
❏ It's Finally Here, Spring…	1	❏ It's What's Next	1
❏ It's Flu Season, So Come Empty Our Coffers	1	❏ It's Your Life, So Live It	1
❏ It's Going on Write Now	1	❏ January Jamboree	1
❏ It's Good!	1	❏ Jam Packed Jelly	1
❏ It's in There	1	❏ Judge Our Books by Their Savings	1
❏ It's Late – Your Kids Are Probably at Our Sale	1	❏ Jump Into Spring	1

1

Sales Term	Misery Meter	Sales Term	Misery Meter
❏ June Is for Junipers & the Rest of Our Trees	1	❏ Knock Down the Walls	1
❏ June Jitterbug – Save on Classic Vinyl	1	❏ Knock, Knock, We're Here	1
❏ Just Be Here, OK?	1	❏ Knock Off Early	1
❏ Just Because	1	❏ Labor Day Weekend	1
❏ Just for You	1	❏ Lasso Your Romeo	1
❏ Just the Faxes	1	❏ Last Blast	1
❏ Just the Kitchen Sink	1	❏ Last Minute	1
❏ Kaboom! Summer Blast Off!	1	❏ Last One in Is Still Very Lucky	1
❏ Keep More Cash For Keepsakes	1	❏ Last Minute Hunting	1
❏ Keep on Truckin'	1	❏ Layaway for Later	1
❏ Keep Step With March Sales	1	❏ Leaf the Discounts to the Pros	1
❏ Keep the Pounds Off	1	❏ Leap on the Deals	1
❏ Keep Your Money at Home	1	❏ Leave the Cash at Home	1
❏ Keep Your Mind on Our Gutters	1	❏ Leave the Neighbors in the Dust	1
❏ Key in to Win	1	❏ Leave the Purse at Home	1
❏ Kick Off the Season With Our	1	❏ Leave the Wallet at Home	1
❏ Kid's Easter	1	❏ Lefthanders	1
❏ Kiss 'N' Sale	1	❏ Lefty	1
		❏ Less Is More	1

Sales Term	Misery Meter	Sales Term	Misery Meter
❏ Let 'Em Look	1	❏ Lots of Lots	1
❏ Let It Ride	1	❏ Love Is Blind, but Our Prices You Can See	1
❏ Let There Be Savings	1		
❏ Let Us Count the Ways	1	❏ Love Lasts Forever, but This Sale Won't	1
❏ Let Us Tell You Where to Stick It	1	❏ Love Thy Sale as Thyself	1
❏ Life Begins at Forty	1	❏ Low Down Subwoofer	1
❏ Life in the Discount Lane	1	❏ Low, Low Sale	1
❏ Linen	1	❏ Lunch Hour	1
❏ Listen to Your Kids	1	❏ Made for You	1
❏ Listen to Your Wife	1	❏ Made in the USA	1
❏ Listen to Your Muse	1	❏ Madness Has Arrived With This	1
❏ Live and Learn	1	❏ Magic of Lights	1
❏ Live for Today	1	❏ Make 'Em Wonder	1
❏ Live the Good Life	1	❏ Make It a Double	1
❏ Live Your Dreams	1	❏ Make It Up to the Kids	1
❏ Lock, Stock, and Barrel	1	❏ Make It Up to the Wife	1
❏ Local Area Code Appreciation	1	❏ Make It Up to Them Later	1
❏ Look What We Found	1	❏ Make It Up to Your Man	1
❏ Look Our Gift Horse in the Mouth	1	❏ Make Room for Baby	1
		❏ Make Room for More	1

Sales Term	Misery Meter	Sales Term	Misery Meter
❏ Make Your Own Instant	1	❏ More Bags for Your Buck	1
❏ Map Your Savings	1	❏ More Bang for Your Buck	1
❏ March Madness	1	❏ More Fool Us	1
❏ Martha's Favorite	1	❏ More for Less	1
❏ Martha's Outta Jail	1	❏ More for the Taking	1
❏ Maxed Out Monday	1	❏ More of It Monday	1
❏ Mega Dittos	1	❏ More Than Just Staples	1
❏ Men's	1	❏ More Than One Is More Fun – and Less!	1
❏ Mercury's Falling	1		
❏ Mid-Winter House Warming	1	❏ Mostly Perfect Stuff	1
❏ Mid-Winter Melt Down	1	❏ Move Over Pentium	1
❏ Mid-Winter's Day	1	❏ Movie Star Mania	1
❏ Might Come in Handy Some Day	1	❏ Mud Season Celebration	1
		❏ Mum's the Word	1
❏ Miles of Smiles	1	❏ Name	1
❏ Million Dollar	1	❏ Nature Loves Our Vacuums	1
❏ Money Doesn't Grow on Trees – Usually	1	❏ Never Clean It Again	1
❏ Money Talks Louder Than Usual	1	❏ Never Gonna Be a Better Time	1
❏ Money Savings	1	❏ Never Say Never	1
❏ Monument	1	❏ New Kid on the Block	1

1

Sales Term	Misery Meter	Sales Term	Misery Meter
❏ New Merchandise	1	❏ Oh the Humanity	1
❏ Nice Guys Finish First	1	❏ Oil's Well That Ends Well	1
❏ Night Into Day	1	❏ Ol' Man Winter	1
❏ No Beatin' Around the Bush	1	❏ Once in a Long While	1
❏ No Bull	1	❏ Old-Time Sale	1
❏ No Cure Beats a Manicure	1	❏ Once in a While	1
❏ No If's, And's, or Butt's	1	❏ Once Upon a Time	1
❏ No More Excuses	1	❏ One Hour	1
❏ No Reason, Just Right	1	❏ One in a Million	1
❏ No Scrooges Allowed	1	❏ One Syllable	1
❏ Not Just Another January	1	❏ Online & Offline Savings	1
❏ Nothing Says Summer Like Our Hot Sales	1	❏ Online Coupon	1
		❏ Only Our Lures Are Fishy	1
❏ November Countdown to the Holidays	1	❏ Only You Know What You Want	1
❏ November Is Novice Month	1	❏ Open Labor Day for This	1
❏ Odd Hour Discounts	1	❏ Opportunity Knocks Only Once	1
❏ Odds & Ends	1		
❏ Off With Our Prices	1	❏ Or Your Money Back	1
❏ Oh Baby, It's Cold Outside	1	❏ Orange Tag	1
❏ Oh Me, Oh My, Oh Romeo	1	❏ Our Back to School Sale Continues	1

Sales Term	Misery Meter	Sales Term	Misery Meter
❏ Our Bargains Are Better Than Bribes	1	❏ Pass on the Savings	1
❏ Our Biggest Fan	1	❏ Pass the Buck (From Us to You!)	1
❏ Our Discounts Make Gnus	1	❏ Patriotic	1
❏ Our Early Snowbird	1	❏ Pay for What You Want	1
❏ Our Fishing Sale Is Gonna Getcha	1	❏ Peek at Our Summer Savings	1
❏ Our Good Sale Is Easy to Find	1	❏ Penniless	1
❏ Our Low Prices Raise the Dead	1	❏ Perfect Patron	1
❏ Our Rugs Will Fly Forever. Our Sale Won't.	1	❏ Pick a Card	1
❏ Our Sweetheart of a Sale	1	❏ Pick a Nose	1
❏ Out of Sight	1	❏ Pick a Number	1
❏ Out of the World Sale	1	❏ Pick a Pair	1
❏ Out to Lunch	1	❏ Pick a Peck of Pickles	1
❏ Outdoor Living Sale	1	❏ Pick & Choose	1
❏ Outta Sight Saturday	1	❏ Pick Your Poison	1
❏ Paint the Town Red	1	❏ Picket Fence	1
❏ Paint Your Way Into the Bargain Corner	1	❏ Pink Elephant	1
		❏ Plantastic Plant	1
❏ Party Line	1	❏ Play on It First	1
		❏ Point, Click, Save	1
		❏ Post Time Is Sale Time	1

Sales Term	Misery Meter	Sales Term	Misery Meter
❏ Pot Shot – Hit It to Win Discounts	1	❏ Read Our Lips	1
❏ Power Savings Hour	1	❏ Read This Sign From the Inside	1
❏ Practice Makes Perfect	1		
❏ Pre-Mother's Day	1	❏ Ready, Aim, Fire Up the Savings	1
❏ Prepared to Be Dazzled by This Amazing Sale	1		
		❏ Red Light	1
❏ Pre-Season	1	❏ Red Ribbon	1
❏ Presidents' Day Two-Day	1	❏ Re-Gift Yourself	1
❏ Pre-Spring inventory Wacky, Wild, Wow	1	❏ Remember September	1
		❏ Rev Up for Shopping Season	1
❏ Pre-Winter Energy	1		
❏ Pre-Winter Sale Is on Now	1	❏ Rhymes With Pail	1
❏ Price Propositions	1	❏ Ring in the New Year	1
❏ Printer Cartridge Blowout	1	❏ Rock the Boat	1
❏ Pull Up a Chair	1	❏ Rock the Vote	1
❏ Pump It Up Athletic	1	❏ Roctober Music Clearance	1
❏ Quarterly _____	1	❏ Romeo Rodeo	1
❏ Race Day	1	❏ Root 'Em On	1
❏ Rake in the Bargains	1	❏ Rotating Special	1
❏ Read Between the Lines	1	❏ Roulette	1
❏ Read 'Em and Weep	1	❏ Royal Flush Bathroom Event	1

Sales Term	Misery Meter	Sales Term	Misery Meter
❑ Rush Hour	1	❑ Screw Your Savings to the Sticking Price	1
❑ Sailing On	1	❑ Scrimp & Save Without the Scrimping	1
❑ Sale for the Faithful	1		
❑ Sales at Sixty Smiles an Hour	1	❑ Scuba Dooba Done	1
❑ Sales Is as Sales Does	1	❑ Season of Joy	1
❑ Same Look for Less	1	❑ Season of Sharing	1
❑ Santa Will Sleigh You	1	❑ Season's Greetings	1
❑ Santa's Sack	1	❑ Secret Word Sale	1
❑ Save Often, Save Early	1	❑ See Change	1
❑ Save Yourself	1	❑ See for Yourself	1
❑ Savings Is the Best Medicine	1	❑ See It Writ Large	1
		❑ See Santa & Save	1
❑ Savor Our Tasty Bargains	1	❑ See the Big Picture	1
❑ Say a Saying and Save	1	❑ See the Game	1
❑ Say Our Name and Save	1	❑ See the Game With Us	1
❑ School Days	1	❑ See Your Soaps While You Shop	1
❑ School Daze	1		
❑ Scotch Hour	1	❑ Seize the August Days Sales Event	1
❑ Scratch & Win	1	❑ Select Item	1
❑ Scratch Off Saturday	1	❑ Sensational Summer	1

Sales Term	Misery Meter	Sales Term	Misery Meter
❏ September Is for Students	1	❏ Shoulda Coulda Woulda	1
❏ Seriously Fun Shopping	1	❏ Show Them the Love	1
❏ Sew It Up	1	❏ Show Up & Save	1
❏ Sex & the City	1	❏ Show Up Your Boss	1
❏ Shape Up for the Season	1	❏ Show Your True Colors	1
❏ Shape Up for the Summer	1	❏ Signs Point to Yes	1
❏ Share Our Air Conditioning	1	❏ Silent Spring	1
❏ Share the Feeling	1	❏ Sing a Song & Save	1
❏ Share Your Secrets With Santa	1	❏ Sister Store	1
❏ Shelf Dusting	1	❏ Sit Down Saturday	1
❏ Shell Out Fewer Clams – Beach Sale	1	❏ Sizzlin' Summer Days	1
❏ Shelter From High Prices	1	❏ Ski Expo	1
❏ Sherry Hour	1	❏ Skin Deep Beauty	1
❏ Shh! We're Hunting Bargains	1	❏ Skip It & You'll Be Sorry	1
❏ Shoes by the Foot	1	❏ Slide Into Something Comfortable	1
❏ Shop Online & Pick It Up Here	1	❏ Slip Into Fall	1
❏ Shore Thing	1	❏ Smart Money Won't Miss This Labor Day	1
❏ Short Short Shorts Sale	1	❏ Smoke Break	1
		❏ Snow Days Discounts	1
		❏ Snow Makers…Snow	1

Sales Term	Misery Meter	Sales Term	Misery Meter
❏ Snow Meter Sale	1	❏ Spontaneous	1
❏ So Good You'll Blush (& Mascara!)	1	❏ Spooky Halloween Favorites at the Sale of a Lifetime	1
❏ So Last Week	1		
❏ So You're Having a Baby	1	❏ Spring Break Recovery	1
❏ Soak Up the Savings On Bathroom Products	1	❏ Spring Break Stock Up	1
❏ Soar Into Savings	1	❏ Spring Car Care	1
❏ Sole Survivor Shoe	1	❏ Spring Fest	1
❏ Soul Train Sunday	1	❏ Spring Fever	1
❏ Some Americans Go Through Life Without Discovering Our Columbus Day Sale!	1	❏ Spring Fever Daze	1
		❏ Spring Fix Up	1
		❏ Spring Garden	1
❏ Sparkling July Summer	1	❏ Spring Into Fitness	1
❏ Special Tune Up	1	❏ Spring Into Our	1
❏ Spectacular Autumn	1	❏ Spring Migration	1
❏ Spin Up Savings on Washers	1	❏ Spring Paint	1
❏ Spoil Him Rotten	1	❏ Spring Riot	1
❏ Spoil Your Sweetheart	1	❏ Spring Splash	1
❏ Spoil Yourself	1	❏ Spring Time-To-Save Time	1
❏ Spoil Yourself Silly	1	❏ Spring's On	1
❏ Spoiled Rotten	1	❏ Spruce Up	1

1

Sales Term	Misery Meter	Sales Term	Misery Meter
❏ Squeaky Wheels Get the Savings	1	❏ Stop Holding Your Breath	1
❏ Squeezable	1	❏ Stop in the Name of Love	1
❏ St. Paddy's Preview	1	❏ Stop Saving – You Can Have It Today	1
❏ Stake Your Claim on Discounts	1	❏ Stop the Dresses	1
❏ Start Saving Now	1	❏ Stop the Presses	1
❏ Start Your Engines	1	❏ Stop Wishing	1
❏ Start Your Engines on Saving	1	❏ Stop, Drop, & Save	1
❏ State Fair	1	❏ Storage Space On	1
❏ Steak Your Claim on Grilles	1	❏ Store Your Stuff	1
❏ Steal a Deal	1	❏ Stork Up for Baby	1
❏ Stellar Savings on Astronomy	1	❏ Storm Daze	1
❏ Stick With Your Day Job – Weekend Extravaganza	1	❏ Straight From the Source	1
❏ Sticker Up	1	❏ Straight Shootin'	1
❏ Still at It	1	❏ Street Lamp	1
❏ Stock the Fridge	1	❏ Stride Into Our Shoe Sale	1
❏ Stock Up for Winter	1	❏ Stringed Things	1
❏ Stock Up on Slow Food	1	❏ Stuck on You	1
❏ Stocking Stuffer	1	❏ Student Appreciation	1
		❏ Student Discount	1
		❏ Stuff	1

Sales Term	Misery Meter	Sales Term	Misery Meter
❏ Stuff Yourself Silly	1	❏ Sun-Sational	1
❏ Stump the Chump	1	❏ Sunset Savings	1
❏ Stump Us & Save	1	❏ Super Autumn Values Are Now On	1
❏ Such Stuff as Dreams Are Made Of	1	❏ Super Car	1
❏ Suck Up the Vacuum Discounts	1	❏ Super Duper Sunday	1
❏ Sudden Sunday	1	❏ Super Presidents'	1
❏ Suicide Hour	1	❏ Super Spring	1
❏ Summer Blast Off	1	❏ Super Summer	1
❏ Summer Camp Stock Up	1	❏ Super Summer Coupon	1
❏ Summer Safari	1	❏ Support Local Businesses	1
❏ Summer Shape Up	1	❏ Support the Right to Armchairs	1
❏ Summer Sale Goes Out in a Blaze of Glory	1	❏ Support Your Local Schools	1
❏ Summer Solstice	1	❏ Surf, Print, & Save	1
❏ Summer Sundays	1	❏ Surprisingly Affordable	1
❏ Summerfest	1	❏ Swap It	1
❏ Summerswap	1	❏ Swap With Us	1
❏ Sunday Sun Splash	1	❏ Sweet Dreams	1
❏ Sunny Sunday	1	❏ Sweetheart of a	1
❏ Sunrise to Sunset	1	❏ Sweets for Your Sweet	1

1

Sales Term	Misery Meter	Sales Term	Misery Meter
❏ Swim Into Sweet Deals	1	❏ Terrible Tuesday	1
❏ Swing Into Spring	1	❏ Terrific Tuesday	1
❏ Swipe Your Card for Savings	1	❏ Texas Hold-em Draw & Save	1
❏ Tailgater Days	1	❏ Thank You	1
❏ Tails You Win Too	1	❏ Thank You for Your Patronage	1
❏ Take a Stand	1	❏ Thanks-For-Giving	1
❏ Take a Walk on the Sale Side of the Street	1	❏ That Time of the Month	1
❏ Take Back the City	1	❏ The "Under There" Event	1
❏ Take Back the Streets	1	❏ The Beef Is Here!	1
❏ Take Big Savings at Our...	1	❏ The Big	1
❏ Take It From the Horses Mouth	1	❏ The Big Easy	1
❏ Take It From Us	1	❏ The Buck Stops Here	1
❏ Take It or Leave It	1	❏ The Buck Stops in Your Wallet	1
❏ Take My Knife, Please	1	❏ The Car Wash Will Come to You	1
❏ Take Off the Pounds but Keep Your Wallet Fat	1	❏ The Darkest Hour Is the Best Time to Get Here	1
❏ Talk Is Cheap – Our Sales Are Cheaper	1	❏ The Eskimos Didn't Want Our Ice...Do You?	1
❏ Taste It First & Save	1	❏ The Female Sale	1
❏ Teach Them to Save Early	1	❏ The Frenzy Sale	1

Sales Term	Misery Meter	Sales Term	Misery Meter
❑ The Fruit of Our Looms	1	❑ The Sales Are Under There! Underwear?	1
❑ The Gang's All Here	1	❑ The Sticker's the Starting Price	1
❑ The Great No-Cut Coupon Sale	1	❑ The Summer of Our Content	1
❑ The Great Spring Sale	1		
❑ The Hair Apparent	1	❑ The Teflon Coupon	1
❑ The Joneses Can't Touch This	1	❑ The Total Spring Sale for Him & Her	1
❑ The Last Best Sale of the Season	1	❑ The Tough Got Going Here	1
❑ The Male Sale	1	❑ The Ultimate Ski	1
❑ The Manufacturer Can Suggest Prices All they Want	1	❑ The Way to a Woman's Heart Is Through Her Jewelry	1
❑ The More You Buy the More You Save	1	❑ The White House White Sale	1
❑ The Other Football	1	❑ The Wind Is Blown Away by Our Hat Sale	1
❑ The Other White Meat	1		
❑ The Right Selection, the Right Sale	1	❑ The Winter Shoe and Boot	1
❑ The Round It Down Round Up	1	❑ There Are Snow Bargains to Be Had	1
❑ The Sales Blitz Is On	1	❑ There Won't Be Another Sale Like This for Years	1
❑ The Sale Is Afoot	1	❑ There's a Party in Our Pants Department	1

1

Sales Term	Misery Meter	Sales Term	Misery Meter
❑ There's Gold in Them There Aisles	1	❑ This Joint Is Jumping	1
❑ There's Many a Slip	1	❑ This One Was Made Just for You	1
❑ There's No Business Like Earning Your Business	1	❑ This One Will Shut 'Em Up	1
❑ There's No Place Like Here	1	❑ This Presidents' Day Sale Is Up for Grabs	1
❑ There's No Place Like It	1	❑ This Sale Is Revolutionary, by George!	1
❑ There's No Place Like Rome	1		
❑ There's No Time Like the Present	1	❑ This Sale Needs You	1
❑ There's Nothing Fishy Here	1	❑ This Sale's on Us	1
❑ These Are the Days	1	❑ This Space for Rent	1
❑ They Didn't Want It, but You Do	1	❑ This 3-Point Play Will Get You to the Big Dance	1
❑ They Score More, You Save More	1	❑ Those Were the Days	1
❑ They're Coming Home	1	❑ Thou Shalt Not Spend (Too Much!)	1
❑ Things Are Looking Up	1	❑ Three Hour	1
❑ Things With Cords	1	❑ Thrills & Chills	1
❑ Think You Can Pass Up a Sale This Great?	1	❑ Throw Out the Book Thursday	1
❑ This & That	1	❑ Tick Tock Clock	1
❑ This Is One Big Cushy	1	❑ Time for a New Clock	1
		❑ Tip of the Hat	1

Sales Term	Misery Meter	Sales Term	Misery Meter
❏ To All Our Sweethearts... Happy Valentine's Day	1	❏ Tuck Into a Tux	1
❏ To Give Is Human, to Save Divine	1	❏ Turnover	1
❏ To Go or Not to Go, That Is the Question	1	❏ Twas the Sale Before Christmas	1
❏ To the Victor Go the Savings	1	❏ Twilight Hour	1
❏ Too Many Cooks Mean Even More Savings	1	❏ Twist Our arm	1
❏ Toner Yourself Up	1	❏ Two Hour	1
❏ Top Gift Ideas	1	❏ United States of Consumerism	1
❏ Top of the Class	1	❏ University Day	1
❏ Top of the Hour	1	❏ Unsafe at Any Speed	1
❏ Top of the Morning	1	❏ Unstick From Snow	1
❏ Top Selling Items	1	❏ Unstick Your Mind	1
❏ Tourist Appreciation	1	❏ Up and Up	1
❏ Trench Coat Sale	1	❏ Up in Smoke	1
❏ Trick or Treat	1	❏ Update Your Wardrobe	1
❏ Triple Crown of Savings	1	❏ Use It or Lose It	1
❏ Triple Threat	1	❏ Vacation Goods	1
❏ Try It, You'll Like Us	1	❏ Vegas Days	1
		❏ Wacky Weekend	1
		❏ Wake Up & Save	1

Sales Term	Misery Meter	Sales Term	Misery Meter
❑ Walk This Way	1	❑ We Got, Got, Got What You Need	1
❑ Walk-in & Save	1	❑ We Know What You Need	1
❑ Wallet Transplant	1	❑ We Labored Hard to Lower Our Prices	1
❑ Wallet Warmdown	1	❑ We Like You! We Really Like You!	1
❑ Warm Up to Winter	1	❑ We Made It	1
❑ Warning: Falling Prices	1	❑ We Remember	1
❑ Washington's Birthday	1	❑ We Salute You	1
❑ Washington's First Birthday	1	❑ We Thought They Said "Hypernate" Abnormally Active Winter Event	1
❑ Waste Not, Want Not	1	❑ We Won't Tell if You Won't	1
❑ Watch the Prices Drop Like Magic	1	❑ We Won't Tell Them It Was on Sale	1
❑ We All Live in a Yellow Super Sale	1	❑ Weak Willed Weekend	1
❑ We All Scream for Ice Cream	1	❑ Wear It Home & Save	1
❑ We Bargained, You Save	1	❑ Wear Your Spac Backwards & Save	1
❑ We Beg to Differ	1	❑ Weekend Wackiness	1
❑ We Can't Contain It	1	❑ Weekend Warrior	1
❑ We Eggcell at Easter Bargains	1	❑ Welcome Back Wednesday	1
❑ We Got Lots	1	❑ Welcome Home	1
❑ We Got Your Bag	1		

NOTES

NOTES

Best Sale and Promotional Ideas by Month

PARADE OF VALUES

JANUARY

January is a fresh start. Every customer in the world is expecting a New Year's Sale – so why not give it to them? Stand out from your competitors by presenting a unique promotion that will get your customers talking and bring them right to your door. From classic January promotions to offbeat holidays like Fruitcake Toss Day, you're sure to find an idea to help you start the new sales year off right!

Classic January Sale Terms

❏ A New Look for a New Year

❏ A Once a Year

❏ A Sale Four Years in the Making
Good on Inauguration Day!

❏ A Very Merry-After Christmas

❏ Annual Pick Your Price Event

❏ Baby New Year Makes Three for One!

❏ Best Deal of the Century

❏ Best Deal of the Decade

❏ Best Deal of the Year

❏ Better Than Last Year's Best

❏ Bigger Than Last Year's Biggest

❏ Break out the Bubbly!

❏ Budget Breakers Sale

❏ Buy This Year's Model at Last Year's Prices

❏ Coming to Our Senses

❏ Days After Christmas

❏ Deal of the Century

❏ Done and Done-er: End of the Year Savings

❏ Dynamite Winter Clearance

❏ Early Bird

❏ End of the Model Year Sale

❏ First Friday Sale

❏ Fourth and Long Bargains
Super Bowl Sunday

- ❏ Get the New Year Started Right
- ❏ Gigantic January
- ❏ Gotta Make Room
- ❏ Guess the Score and It's Free *Super Bowl Sunday*
- ❏ Happy New Year!
- ❏ Holiday Hangover Sale
- ❏ Holiday Overstock Clearance
- ❏ Holiday Wrap Up Sale
- ❏ How Else Can We Say Thanks
- ❏ I "Voted" for Discounts *Inauguration Day!*
- ❏ It Only Happens Once a Year Sales Spectacular
- ❏ January 1 Sale – Our Biggest Sale of the Year So Far!
- ❏ Kick Off the New Year
- ❏ Kick Off the Season
- ❏ Last Blast Sale
- ❏ Make Room for New Stock
- ❏ Making Room for What's Next
- ❏ Making Space Sale
- ❏ New Start Sale
- ❏ New Year's Extravaganza

- ❏ Not Just Another January
- ❏ Oh, Baby! It's Cold Outside!
- ❏ Ol' Man Winter
- ❏ One for the History Books
- ❏ Our Annual Winter Sales Event
- ❏ Our Way of Saying Thanks
- ❏ Our Very-Merry After Christmas Sale
- ❏ Out with the Old, In with the New
- ❏ Out with the Old Packaging
- ❏ Party Time
- ❏ Pick the Score and the Item Is Yours *Super Bowl Sunday*
- ❏ Post-Christmas Closeout
- ❏ Profit from Our Misery
- ❏ Rack Clearing
- ❏ Re-gift Yourself
- ❏ Resolve to Save
- ❏ Resolve to Save Money
- ❏ Ring in an Incredible Deal
- ❏ Ring in The New Year
- ❏ Royal Flush Bathroom Event *Thomas Crapper Day is January 27!*

- ❏ Sale of the Century
- ❏ Santa's Sidewalk Sale
- ❏ Save Early, Save Often
- ❏ Season Ending Blowout
- ❏ Shape Up and Save
- ❏ Smart Start for a New Year
- ❏ Snow Days Discount
- ❏ Soak Up the Savings on Bathroom Products *Thomas Crapper Day is January 27!*
- ❏ So Low It's Gonna Hurt
- ❏ So Low We Can't Advertise It
- ❏ Start Saving Now
- ❏ Start the Year Off Right
- ❏ Stock Turnover
- ❏ Take off the pounds, but keep your wallet fat!
- ❏ The Sale You've Been Waiting For
- ❏ This Is Our Final, Final, Final Sale
- ❏ The Other Football *Super Bowl Sunday*
- ❏ The year to forget…a sale to remember!

- ❏ There Are Snow Bargains to Be Had
- ❏ They Score More, You Save More *Super Bowl Sunday*
- ❏ This Year's Fashions at Last Year's Prices
- ❏ Ticket to Savings Sale
- ❏ Truckload Sale
- ❏ Warm Up to Our Winter Bargains
- ❏ We Have No Room Sale
- ❏ We Need the Space
- ❏ We're Overstocked So We're Underpricing
- ❏ We've Got What Santa Forgot
- ❏ When It Snows You Save
- ❏ Who Needs Christmas Wrap in January
- ❏ Winter Carnival
- ❏ Winter Luau
- ❏ Winter Madness
- ❏ Winter Products at Summer Prices
- ❏ Winter Wonderland
- ❏ Winter Workout
- ❏ Yes, It Has Frozen Over

Promotions & Events
To Celebrate For January

- ❏ Book Blitz Month
- ❏ Coffee Gourmet Month
- ❏ Family Fit Lifestyle Month
- ❏ Financial Wellness Month
- ❏ Hot Tea Month
  Come in for a cuppa...stay for the great deals!
- ❏ International Business Success Resolutions Month
- ❏ International Creativity Month
- ❏ International Life Balance Month
- ❏ International Quality of Life Month
- ❏ International Wealth Mentality Month
- ❏ Jump Out of Bed Month
  Give your first 50 customers a great discount!

- ❏ National Be-On Purpose Month
- ❏ National Blood Donor Month
  Give Blood Today? Enjoy Our Thank You Savings!
- ❏ National Cancer Prevention Month
- ❏ National Clean Up Your Computer Month
- ❏ MonthFIS Snowboard World Championship
- ❏ Anchorage Fur Rendezvous
- ❏ Paris-Dakar Endurance Rally
  Get Great Deals Without Driving Halfway Around the World
- ❏ The Miss America Pageant
- ❏ The Monte Carlo Automobile Race
- ❏ Rose Bowl Parade
- ❏ Super Bowl
  Leave him at home and enjoy a Sports Free Shopping Spree!

Coffee Gourmet Month

- ❏ FIS Alpine Ski World Championships
- ❏ National Get Organized Month
- ❏ National Glaucoma Awareness Month
  Can you see our awesome discounts?
- ❏ National High Tech Month
- ❏ National Hobby Month
- ❏ National Mail Order Gardening Month
- ❏ National Mentoring Month
- ❏ National Oatmeal Month
- ❏ National Personal Self-Defense Awareness Month
- ❏ National Reaching Your Potential Month
- ❏ National Returns Month
- ❏ National Soup Month
- ❏ National Yours, Mine, and Ours Month – celebrating step-families
- ❏ Senior Women's Travel Month
- ❏ Walk Your Pet Month
  Bring in your pet promotion!
- ❏ Wolf Moon

Promotions & Events
To Celebrate For January By Week

- ❏ Celebration of Life Week . . . . January 1-7
- ❏ Diet Resolutions Week. . . . . January 1-7
- ❏ New Year's Resolutions Week . . . . January 1-7
- ❏ National Thank-Your-Customers . . . . January 3-7
- ❏ Someday We'll Laugh About This Week . . . . January 3-7
  But right now these deep discounts have us crying!
- ❏ Universal Letter Writing Week . . . . January 3-9
- ❏ Women's Self Empowerment Week . . . . January 3-9

❏ Home Office Safety and Security Week . . . . January 9-15
Have you hugged your shredder today?

❏ Intimate Apparel Week . . . . January 10-14

❏ Cuckoo Dancing – celebrating Laurel &Hardy . . . . . . January 11-17

❏ International Thank-You Days . . . . January 11-18

❏ Habitat for Humanity Week. . . . . January 14-17

❏ National Fresh Squeezed Juice Week . . . . January 15-19

❏ National Skating Week . . . . January 15-23
Slide into Savings Promotion

❏ Healthy Weight Week . . . . January 16-22

❏ Hunt for Happiness Week . . . . January 16-22
Come in Camo and Save 25%!

❏ International Printing Week . . . . January 16-22

❏ Leadership Week International. . . . . January 23-29

❏ National Handwriting Analysis Week . . . . January 23-29
*Can you read this doctor's handwriting?
Get it right and win a prize!*

❏ National Take Back Your Time Week . . . . January 24-28

❏ Solo-Prenuring Week . . . . January 25-29

❏ International Hoof Care Week. . . . . January 26-29
*Not just for horses anymore!
Trot on in for deep discounts!*

❏ All That Jazz. January 30-February 1

❏ Catholic Schools Week . . . . January 30-February 5

❏ Children's Authors and Illustrators . . . . January 31-February 4

Promotions & Events
To Celebrate For January By Day

❑ New Year's Day . . . . January 1

❑ Universal Hour of Peace . . . . January 1
Sixty minutes of stress-free shopping!

❑ Z Day . . . . January 1

❑ Happy Mew Year for Cats . . . . January 2

❑ Fruitcake Toss Day . . . . January 3

❑ National Write to Congress Day. . . . . January 3
A great day to discount things that don't work!

❑ Trivia Day . . . . January 4

❑ National Smith Day . . . . January 6

❑ I'm Not Going to Take It Anymore Day . . . . January 7

❑ National Joy Germ Day. . . . . January 8

❑ Show and Tell Day at Work Day . . . . January 8
*Warn your sales staff – show and tell day is not the
X-rated fun as it sounds like!*

❑ National Clean Off Your Desk Day. . . . . January 10

❑ National Cut Your Energy Costs Day . . . . January 10

❑ Organize Your Home Day . . . . January 10

❑ Thank God It's Monday Day . . . . January 10

❑ Weigh-In Day . . . . January 10

❑ Penguin Appreciation Day. . . . . January 15
Great time for a Black and White Promotion!

❑ Bald Eagle Appreciation Day . . . . January 15-16

❑ Appreciate a Dragon Day . . . . January 16

❑ National Nothing Day Day. . . . . January 16

❑ Customer Service Day . . . . January 17

❑ Judgment Day . . . . January 17
  Have a Schwarzenegger Impression Contest!

❑ Martin Luther King Jr. Day . . . . January 17

❑ Rid the World of Fad Diets & Gimmicks . . . . January 18

❑ Get To Know Your Customers Day. . . . . January 20

❑ Women's Healthy Weight Day . . . . January 20

❑ National Hugging Day . . . . January 21
  *Contest best hugger in town

❑ Squirrel Appreciation Day . . . . January 21
  A free pound of cashews with every purchase!

❑ Answer Your Cat's Question Day . . . . January 22

❑ National Handwriting Day . . . . January 23
  (sponsor a contest)

❑ Snowplow Mailbox Hockey Day . . . . January 23

❑ Better Business Communication Day . . . . January 24

❑ A Room of One's Own Day . . . . January 25

❑ National Speak Up and Succeed Day. . . . . January 25

❑ National Compliment Day. January 26
  Give discount for anyone that give a compliment

❑ Thomas Crapper Day . . . . January 27
  Ideal for Plumbing Promotions

Birthdays To Celebrate In January
(Can be used for either price or non price promotions)

❏ J. Edgar Hoover . . . . January 1
Our great deals are no secret!

❏ Isaac Asimov . . . . January 2

❏ Mel Gibson . . . . January 3

❏ JRR Tolkien . . . . January 3

❏ Charlie Rose . . . . January 5

❏ Diane Keaton . . . . January 5

❏ Katie Couric . . . . January 7

❏ Nicholas Cage . . . . January 7

❏ Elvis Presley . . . . January 8
Enter our Elvis Impersonator Contest

❏ Bob Eubanks . . . . January 8

❏ Soupy Sales . . . . January 8

❏ Richard Nixon . . . . January 9
*We're not crooks…but you'll feel like one after the
sweet steal of deal you'll get today!*

❏ Joan Baez . . . . January 9
Can't believe she has the same birthday as Nixon

❏ Rod Stewart . . . . January 10

❏ Mary Bilge . . . . January 11

❏ Howard Stern . . . . January 12

❏ Rush Limbaugh. . . . . January 12
*Rush Limbaugh and Howard Stern share the
same birthday? Now that you know that, I'll bet you'll
never look at your radio the same way again!*

❏ Jim Carrey . . . . January 17

❏ Maury Povich . . . . January 17

❏ Kevin Costner . . . . January 18

❏ AA Milne. . . . . January 18
Winnie the Pooh Promotions Galore!

❏ Dolly Parton. . . . . January 19
This Sale's Too Big To Be Believed!

❏ Bill Maher . . . . January 20

❏ Telly Savalas. . . . . January 21
Free lollipop with every purchase!

❏ Neil Diamond . . . . January 24

❏ Ellen DeGeneres . . . . January 26

❏ Paul Newman. . . . . January 26

❏ Mikhail Baryshnikov . . . . January 27

❏ Oprah Winfrey . . . . January 29
Anything with Oprah is a winner

❏ Dick Cheney. . . . . January 30
Great for a gun or hunting shop

**Chase's Calendar of Events has even more
events, festivals and celebrations!**

NOTES

FEBRUARY

For a short month, February manages to pack in a lot of celebrating. Retailers can go wild with Valentines Day and Presidents Day promotions, or choose for some less well known days. Louis Comfort Tiffany's birthday is a natural for sellers of antiques and fine furniture, while Jell-O Week can get the culinary types jiggling with excitement!

Classic February Sale Terms

- ❏ All American President's Day Sale
- ❏ All That Glitters Is Not Gold – We've Got Diamonds Too
- ❏ All You Need Is Love
- ❏ A President's Day Sale You've Never Seen
- ❏ Beyond Excitement
- ❏ Bold Gold
- ❏ Buy Your Happiness
- ❏ Capture the Feeling
- ❏ Capture the Moment
- ❏ Come in Out of the Cold
- ❏ Cupid's on Strike Promotion
- ❏ Cupid Sale

- ❏ Cupid Strikes
- ❏ Don't Deny Your Urges
- ❏ Don't Disappoint Her
- ❏ Everything for Your Honey
- ❏ Everything Red
- ❏ For Better or For Best
- ❏ For Better or For Worse
- ❏ For the Love of _____ Sale
- ❏ For Your One in a Million Girl
- ❏ Gather Ye Roses...and Give Them to Her
- ❏ Gem (and Jewel) of a Sale
- ❏ Get What You Really Wanted
- ❏ Get Your Gift for Juliet Yet?
- ❏ Grab Your Girl and Go

- ❏ Grab Your Guy and Go
- ❏ His and Hers
- ❏ Honest Abe Says
- ❏ Honest Abe Can't Believe These Prices
- ❏ How Many Candles Will These Presidents Be Blowing Out During Our Blow Out?
- ❏ Hot Deals for Cold Months
- ❏ It's the One You've Been Waiting For
- ❏ Just Because
- ❏ Kiss'N Sale
- ❏ Lasso Your Romeo
- ❏ Last Blast
- ❏ Last Minute
- ❏ Love Is Blind, but Our Prices You Can See
- ❏ Love Lasts Forever, but This Sale Won't
- ❏ Love Thy Sale as Thyself
- ❏ Lover's Sale
- ❏ More Than One Is More Fun – and Less!
- ❏ Never Gonna Be a Better Time
- ❏ Nice Guys Finish First
- ❏ Oh, Baby, It's Cold Outside
- ❏ Oh Me, Oh My, Oh Romeo
- ❏ One in a Million
- ❏ Only You Know What Your Want
- ❏ Our Sweetheart of a Sale
- ❏ Paint the Town Red
- ❏ President's Day Two-Day Event
- ❏ Romeo Rodeo
- ❏ Save Lots of Lincoln's and Plenty of Washington's During Our President's Day Sale
- ❏ Share the Feeling
- ❏ Shop in the Name of Love
- ❏ Show Them the Love
- ❏ Ski Expo
- ❏ Skip It and You'll Be Sorry
- ❏ Spoil Him Rotten
- ❏ Spoiled Rotten
- ❏ Spoil Your Sweetheart
- ❏ Spoil Yourself
- ❏ Spoil Yourself Silly
- ❏ State of the Antique *Tiffany's Birthday is February 18*
- ❏ Stop Wishing

- Stuck on You
- Such Sales as Dreams Are Made Of
- Super President's Day Promotion
- Sweet Dreams
- Sweetheart of a Sale
- Sweets for Your Sweet
- There Won't Be Another Sale Like This for Years! *Great for Leap Day*
- There's a Party in Our Pants Department
- There's Gold in Them There Aisles
- The Sales Are Under There. Underwear?
- The Way to a Woman's Heart Is Through Her Jewelry
- The White House White Elephant Sale
- This President's Day Sale Is Up for Grabs
- This Sale Is Revolutionary… by George!
- To All Our Sweethearts… Happy Valentine's Day

- Top Gift Ideas
- Washington's Birthday
- Washington's First Birthday
- We'll Treat You with Dignity During Our President's Day
- We're Wedded to Bargains
- We've Got What Your Romeo Really Wants
- We've Got Your Bed Covered
- We Won't Tell Her It Was on Sale
- When Only the Finest Will Do
- Whoops! Here it is again!
- Who Loves You, Baby?
- Who Says You Can't Buy Happiness?
- Wild Weekend
- Wishes Come True Wednesday
- Yield to Your Urges
- You Can't Buy Love, but You Can Buy _____
- You'll Love It
- You're Invited to the President's Ball
- You're the Authority on Our President's Day

Promotions & Events
To Celebrate For February

- ❏ American Heart Month
- ❏ Back for Family Fun Month
- ❏ Black History Month
- ❏ Fabulous Florida Strawberry Month
- ❏ International Boost Self Esteem Month
- ❏ International Expect Success Month
- ❏ Library Lovers Month
- ❏ National African American History Month
- ❏ National Caffeine Addiction Awareness Month *Great time to discount fruit juices, herbal teas, and dairy drinks!*
- ❏ National Cherry Pie Month
- ❏ National Children's Dental Health Month
- ❏ National Hot Breakfast Month
- ❏ National Parent Leadership Month
- ❏ National Pet Dental Health Month
- ❏ National Time Management Month
- ❏ National Weddings Month
- ❏ North Carolina Sweet Potato Month
- ❏ Plant the Seeds of Greatness Month
- ❏ Relationship Wellness Month *Buy one for yourself, get one for your sweetie half off!*
- ❏ Return Shopping Carts to the Supermarket Month
- ❏ Snow Moon Month
- ❏ Wise Health Care Consumer Month
- ❏ Youth Leadership Month
- ❏ Chinese New Year
- ❏ Nextel Cup Racing Season Kick Off
- ❏ Bullnanza!
- ❏ Pebble Beach National Pro-Am Golf Tournament
- ❏ The America's Cup
- ❏ FIS Ski Jumping World Championships
- ❏ Missouri Mid-Winter Bluegrass Festival

Promotions & Events
To Celebrate For February By Week

❑ Publicity for Profit Week. February 1-7

❑ Women's Heart Week . . . . February 1-7

❑ Get Paid to Shop Week. February 6-12

❑ International Coaching Week . . . . February 6-12

❑ National School Counseling Week . . . . February 7-11

❑ Freelance Writer's Appreciation Week . . . . February 7-12

❑ Boy Scout Anniversary Week . . . . February 8-14
    Wear your uniform to the store, get half off!

❑ Jell-O Week . . . . February 13-19

❑ Celebration of Love Week . . . . February 13-19

❑ Heart Failure Awareness Week . . . . February 13-19

❑ International Flirting Week . . . . February 14-20

❑ National Condom Week . . . . February 14-21

❑ Random Acts of Kindness Week . . . . February 14-20

❑ International Friendship Week . . . . February 20-26

❑ National Engineers Week . . . . February 20-26
    *Toys for Tomorrow's Engineers Today –
    Deep Discounts on Erector Sets!*

❑ Live to Give Week . . . . February 21-27

❑ Read Me Week . . . . February 28-March 4

Promotions & Events
To Celebrate For February By Day

- ❏ Robinson Crusoe Day . . . . .February 1

- ❏ Women's Heart Health Day . . . . .February 1

- ❏ African American Coaches Day . . . . .February 2

- ❏ Groundhog Day . . . . .February 2
  If Punxsutawney Phil Sees His Shadow, Everyone Saves Big!

- ❏ Groundhog Job Shadow Day . . . . .February 2

- ❏ Self Renewal Day . . . . .February 2

- ❏ Wear Red Day . . . . .February 4

- ❏ USO Day . . . . .February 4
  Buy One Bob Hope Movie, Get One Free!

- ❏ Weatherman's Day . . . . .February 5

- ❏ Pay a Compliment Day . . . . .February 6

- ❏ Wave All Your Fingers at Your Neighbor Day . . . . .February 7
  Great Deals on Fencing

❑ Ferris Wheel Day . . . . .February 14

❑ National Have a Heart Day . . . . .February 14

❑ Race Relations Day . . . . .February 14

❑ Quirky Alone Day . . . . .February 14

❑ Susan B. Anthony Day . . . . .February 15

❑ My Way Day . . . . .February 17

❑ National PTA Founder's Day . . . . .February 17

❑ World Human Spirit Day .February 17

❑ Northern Hemisphere Hoodie Hoo Day . . . . .February 20
   Join Us At High Noon to Holler Hoodie Hoo and Scare Winter Away!

❑ International Mother Language Day . . . . .February 21

❑ President's Day . . . . .February 21

❑ For the Love of Mike Day .February 22
   Is Your Name Mike? Come in for 10% off!

❑ Spay Day. . . . . .February 22

❑ Curling Is Cool Day . . . . .February 23
   Discount Brooms and Hairspray — Everybody Wins!

❑ Introduce a Girl to Engineering Day . . . . .February 24

❑ For Pete's Sake Day . . . . .February 26
   Is Your Name Pete? Come in for 10% off!

❑ Floral Design Day . . . . .February 28

❑ Leap Day. . . . . , ...February 29
   Prices so low they come only once every four years!

Birthdays To Celebrate In February
(Can be used for either price or non price promotions)

- [ ] Lisa Marie Presley . . . . .February 1

- [ ] Oscar De La Hoya . . . . .February 4

- [ ] Alice Cooper . . . . .February 4
  Classic Rock Promotions

- [ ] Dan Quayle . . . . .February 4

- [ ] Chris Rock . . . . .February 7

- [ ] Garth Brooks . . . . .February 7

- [ ] Charles Dickens . . . . .February 7
  Please, sir, can we have some more…great prices?

- [ ] Alice Walker . . . . .February 9
  Everything Purple On Sale!

- [ ] Thomas Edison . . . . February 11

- [ ] Abraham Lincoln . . . . February 12

- [ ] Judy Blume . . . . February 12

- [ ] Arsenio Hall . . . . February 12

- [ ] Jerry Springer . . . . February 13

- [ ] LeVar Burton . . . . February 16

- [ ] Michael Jordan . . . . February 17

- [ ] Paris Hilton . . . . February 17
  Great for "Win a Shopping Spree" Promotions

- [ ] Dr. Dre . . . . February 18

❑ Louis Comfort Tiffany . . . . February 18
Antique Dealers, this one's for you!

❑ Vanna White . . . . February 18

❑ Jack Palance . . . . February 18

❑ Sidney Poitier . . . . February 20

❑ Jeri Ryan . . . . February 22

❑ Steve "The Crocodile Hunter" Irwin . . . . February 22
Save on all leather goods

❑ George Washington . . . . February 22

❑ Johnny Cash . . . . February 26
Walk the Line...to Great Prices!

❑ Levi Strauss . . . . February 26

❑ Elizabeth Taylor . . . . February 27

❑ Ralph Nader . . . . February 27
Do you think Ralph and Liz celebrate together?

❑ Jeff "Ja Rule" Atkins . . . . February 29

**Chase's Calendar of Events has even more
events, festivals and celebrations!**

NOTES

_____

_____

_____

_____

_____

_____

_____

_____

_____

_____

_____

_____

_____

_____

_____

_____

_____

MARCH

You won't need the "Luck of the Irish" to come up with great promotional ideas this month! From March Madness to Spring Cleaning, there are dozens of sales opportunities for the savvy retailer to pick from. Don't miss the humor celebrations – a laughing customer is a happy customer.

Classic March Sale Terms

- ❏ Acres of Spring Savings
- ❏ A Spring Sale So Hot You'll Think It's Summer
- ❏ Bracket Busted? So's Our Prices!
- ❏ Bring On the Season
- ❏ Build Your Dream _____ at Our Spring Fever Sale
- ❏ Buy Two Rabbits, Get More For Free!
- ❏ Clean Out Your Closet
- ❏ Clean Up on Spring
- ❏ Clean Up on Detergents and Cleansers
- ❏ Dust to Dust Housecleaning
- ❏ Fall in Love with Freebies

- ❏ Fresh Fashion
- ❏ Frozen Goods Fridays
- ❏ Get Ready for Bikini Season
- ❏ Get Set for Spring
- ❏ Gotta Make Room!
- ❏ Great Minds Shop Here
- ❏ Guess the Score and It's Free
- ❏ Hems Are Rising, Prices Are Falling
- ❏ Home Improvement
- ❏ Home Office Upgrade
- ❏ Hoops Forever
- ❏ If You're In, You Win
- ❏ In Like a Lion, Out Like a Lamb

- ❏ It's Finally Here...
  Spring _____
- ❏ It's Not a Typo
- ❏ Jump Into Spring
- ❏ Keep Step with the March
  Savings
- ❏ Keep Your Mind on Our Gutters
- ❏ Kick Off the Season
  with _____
- ❏ Madness Has Arrived with This
- ❏ Make It Up to the Wife
- ❏ March Madness
- ❏ March Masquerade
- ❏ Mark-Down Madness Sale
- ❏ More Than Just Staples
  *Organize Your Home
  Office Week*
- ❏ Name Your Price Sale
- ❏ Nature Loves Our Vacuums
- ❏ Old Fashioned Spring Sale
- ❏ Our Low Prices Raise the Dead
- ❏ Pick the Score and the Item
  Is Yours
- ❏ Pre-Season
- ❏ Pre-Spring Inventory:
  Wacky, Wild, Wow!

- ❏ Prices Are Melting During Our
  Spring Thaw
- ❏ Quarterly _____
- ❏ Race Day
- ❏ Root 'Em On
- ❏ Score One for the Little Guys
- ❏ See the Game with Us
- ❏ Sew Up Great Savings
  National Craft Month
- ❏ Shameless Spring Savings
- ❏ Shape Up for the Season
- ❏ Shape Up for the Summer
- ❏ Silent Spring
- ❏ Spin the Spring Savings Wheel
- ❏ Spring Break Recovery
- ❏ Spring Break Stock Up
- ❏ Spring Car Care
- ❏ Spring Fest
- ❏ Spring Fever
- ❏ Spring Fever Daze
- ❏ Spring Fix-Up
- ❏ Spring Fling
- ❏ Spring Gala
- ❏ Spring Garden
- ❏ Spring Into Fitness

- ❏ Spring Into Our _____
- ❏ Spring Into Shape
- ❏ Spring Jubilee
- ❏ Spring Migration
  *Grab the Good Deals
  Before They Fly Away!*
- ❏ Spring Paint
- ❏ Spring Pilgrimage
- ❏ Spring Price Buster
- ❏ Spring Remodeling
  Clearance
- ❏ Spring Riot
- ❏ Spring Savings
- ❏ Spring Spectacular
- ❏ Spring Splash
- ❏ Spring Tent
- ❏ Spring Time-To-Save-Time
- ❏ St. Paddy's Preview
- ❏ Steak Your Claim on Grilles
- ❏ Stellar Savings on Astronomy
- ❏ Stop the Madness
- ❏ Suck Up the Vacuum
  Discounts
  *National Cleaning Week
  Promotion!*

- ❏ Super Spring
- ❏ Swing Into Spring
- ❏ Talk Is Cheap – Our Sales Are
  Cheaper
  *Great for Alexander Graham
  Bell's Birthday*
- ❏ The Great Spring Sale
- ❏ The Temperature Goes Up…
  Our Prices Come Down!
- ❏ The Total Spring Sale for Him
  and Her
- ❏ They Score More, You Save More
  Great for March Madness
- ❏ Too Much Stuff
- ❏ Top of the Morning
- ❏ Update Your Wardrobe
- ❏ We Don't Want to Count
  It…Spring Inventory Sale
- ❏ West of the Rest
  *Great for L'Amour and Wyatt
  Earp Birthdays!*
- ❏ Who Authorized This Sale?
- ❏ You Can Dig It with Our Yard
  Tools
- ❏ You Can Have It All
- ❏ You Shoot, You Score a Discount

Promotions & Events
To Celebrate For March

- American Red Cross Month

- Deaf History Month

- Financial Security Month

- Health Care Diversity Month

- Honor Society Awareness Month
Bring in a Good Report Card Promotion

- Humorists Are Artists Month

- International Idea Month

- International Listening Awareness Month

- International Mirth Month

- Irish American Heritage Month
Save Some Green While Wearing Green!

- Music in Our Schools Month

- National Athletic Training Month

- National Caffeine Awareness Month

- National Craft Month

- National Frozen Food Month

- Iditarod Dog Race

- Great American Meat Out

- Academy Awards

- March Madness: NCAA Final Four

- Miami Grand Prix

- National Nutrition Month

- National On-Hold Month

- National Talk to Your Teen About Sex Month
Wouldn't you rather be shopping?

- National Umbrella Month

- National Women's History Month

- Optimism Month

- Play the Recorder Month
Headache Remedies Half Off!

- Poison Prevention Month
Great Time to Discount Home Safety Items

- Save Your Vision Month

- Small Press Month

Promotions & Events
To Celebrate For March By Week

❑ Newspapers in Education Week . . . . March 1-5

❑ National Cheerleading Week . . . . March 1-7

❑ Return the Borrowed Books Week . . . . March 1-7
Isn't It Time to Buy Your Own Copy?

❑ Universal Human Beings Week . . . . March 1-7

❑ Write a Letter of Appreciation Week . . . . March 1-7

❑ Celebrate Your Name Week . . . . March 6-12

❑ National Girl Scout Week . . . . March 6-12
Wear Your Uniform for Deep Discounts!

❑ Save Your Vision Week . . . . March 6-12

❑ Help Someone See Week . . . . March 6-13

❑ National School Breakfast Week . . . . March 7-11

❑ National Procrastination Week . . . . March 7-13
Come in at the end of the day and save more!

❑ Universal Women's Week . . . . March 8-14

❑ Campfire USA Birthday Week . . . . March 14-20

❑ International Brain Awareness Week . . . . March 14-20

❑ Severe Weather Awareness Week . . . . March 17-23
Stock Up Now on Emergency Supplies

❑ National Agriculture Week . . . . March 20-26

❑ National Massage Safety Week . . . . March 20-26

❑ National Spring Fever Week . . . . March 20-26

Promotions & Events
To Celebrate For March By Day

Birthdays To Celebrate In March
(Can be used for either price or non price promotions)

❑ Ron Howard . . . . March 1

❑ Jon Bon Jovi. . . . . March 2

❑ Dr. Seuss. . . . . March 2

❑ Alexander Graham Bell . . . . March 3
Great Day for a Phone Sale!

❑ Shaquille O'Neal . . . . March 6

❑ Elizabeth Barrett Browning . . . . March 6
All Poetry Promotion

❑ Ed McMahon . . . . March 6

❑ Bow Wow . . . . March 9

❑ Chuck Norris. . . . . March 10

❑ Douglas Adams. . . . . March 11
*42 Items in This Store Will Be on Sale –
Great for High Tech Types*

❑ Liza Minnelli . . . . March 12

❑ L. Ron Hubbard . . . . March 13
Tom Cruise Movies Half Off!

❑ Quincy Jones . . . . March 14

❑ Albert Einstein . . . . March 14

❑ Eva Longoria . . . . March 15

❑ Andrew Jackson . . . . March 15
$20 Promotions

❏ Jerry Lewis . . . . March 16

❏ Chuck Woolery . . . . March 16

❏ Queen Latifah. . . . . March 18

❏ Wyatt Earp . . . . March 19
Wild West Savings!

❏ JS Bach. . . . . March 21

❏ Rosie O'Donnell. . . . . March 21

❏ William Shatner . . . . March 22

❏ Louis L'Amour. . . . . March 22
Cowboy Cash

❏ Harry Houdini. . . . . March 24

❏ Elton John. . . . . March 25
If it has sequins, it's on sale!

❏ Gloria Steinem . . . . March 25
If it needs sequins, it's on sale!

❏ Leonard Nimoy . . . . March 26

❏ Mariah Carey . . . . March 27

❏ Vincent Van Gogh . . . . March 30
Buy One Earring, Get One Free!

❏ Ewan McGregor. . . . . March 31

❏ Al Gore. . . . . March 31

**Chase's Calendar of Events has even more
events, festivals and celebrations!**

NOTES

_____

_____

_____

_____

_____

_____

_____

_____

_____

_____

_____

_____

_____

_____

_____

_____

_____

_____

APRIL

April is full of promotional possibilities, and that's no April Fool's Joke. You've got Easter, Tax Day, and a host of other events to celebrate. Jay Leno, David Letterman and Conan O'Brien all share birthdays this month – why not keep the store open till midnight and enjoy the Kings of Late Night?

Classic April Sale Terms

- ❏ A Sale for Everything and Everything Is on Sale
- ❏ A Spring Sale So Hot You'll Think It's Summer
- ❏ A Tisket, a Tasket, Easter Treats for Your Basket
- ❏ After Midnight
- ❏ All Merchandise Is Reduced for Our Giant, Storewide Spring Sales Event
- ❏ Annual Easter Extravaganza
- ❏ April Showers Bring Discounts for Gardeners
- ❏ Baskets of Bargains
- ❏ Best Price in Town
- ❏ Book Your Own Adventure
- ❏ Books By the Pound
- ❏ Be the One They Envy
- ❏ Breathe in the Savings
- ❏ Bunnies and Chicks for Cheep
- ❏ Buy It, You'll Like It
- ❏ Buy Two, Get Two Free
- ❏ Buy Now, Pay Later
- ❏ Buy Yours, Get Theirs for Less *Great for Sibling Day*
- ❏ Caution! Deep Discounts Ahead!
- ❏ Call It Whatever You Want
- ❏ Corner the Market on Spring Produce
- ❏ Don't Pay Till Next Year
- ❏ Don't Tell Mom

- ❑ Don't Tell the Tax Man
- ❑ Double Your Refund
- ❑ Easter Parade
- ❑ Easter's Best
- ❑ Eggcellent Easter Discounts
- ❑ Eggstraordinarily Special Easter
- ❑ Even the Bunny Can't Believe the Bargains
- ❑ Expect the Unexpected
- ❑ Flattery Will Get You Discounts
- ❑ Focus on Saving More
- ❑ Free From Taxes Friday
- ❑ Get It for Less
- ❑ Get Set for Spring
- ❑ Good for the Soul Sunday
- ❑ Great Deals – No Waiting
- ❑ Great Goods for Grandparents
- ❑ Great Memories for Less
- ❑ Guaranteed Lowest Prices of the Year
- ❑ Ham It Up for Easter
- ❑ Happy Easter

- ❑ Here's a Sale That's Just Ducky
- ❑ Hoe Hoe Hoe! Get Your Garden Goods Early!
- ❑ Holiday Wrap-Up
- ❑ Home for the Holiday
- ❑ Hunting for a Great Easter Sale? You've Found It!
- ❑ Ignore the Tags
- ❑ In the Beginning Was the Sale
- ❑ Instant Savings
- ❑ Invest Your Refund
- ❑ Invitation Only
- ❑ It's Going on Write Now *Write Your Memoirs Day*
- ❑ It's Your Rainy Day
- ❑ Jump Into Spring Savings
- ❑ Just Ducky Sale
- ❑ Keep More Cash for Keepsakes
- ❑ Kid's Easter Sale
- ❑ Let Us Pay the Tax – You've Paid Enough!
- ❑ Live the Good Life
- ❑ Low, Low Prices
- ❑ Luxury for Less

- ❏ Midnight Madness
- ❏ Money Doesn't Grow on Trees – Usually!
- ❏ Money Tree
- ❏ More Bang for Your Buck
- ❏ Movie Star Mania *Jack Nicholson's Birthday*
- ❏ No Hype, No Gimmicks Sale
- ❏ No Tax
- ❏ Not for the Timid
- ❏ Open Late
- ❏ Outta Site Saturday
- ❏ Parade of Easter Savings
- ❏ Prices Lower Than the Titanic
- ❏ Print It at Home, Save Here *Great for Electronic Communications Week!*
- ❏ Rock Bottom Sale
- ❏ Rolling Back the Prices
- ❏ Secret Coupon Sale
- ❏ Seriously Fun Shopping
- ❏ Sing a Song and Save *National Karaoke Week!*
- ❏ Stick Us with the Sales Tax
- ❏ Spruce-Up Season Is Here

- ❏ Take a Tax Holiday
- ❏ Tax Free
- ❏ Tax Freedom
- ❏ The Great Spring Sale
- ❏ The Rainy Day Is Here
- ❏ The Road to Savings Is Paved with Our Coupons
- ❏ The Sale Blitz Is On
- ❏ This Sale Is So Good We're Throwing a Party
- ❏ Valued Customers Only
- ❏ VIP Sale
- ❏ We Love Our Customers
- ❏ We Must Be Crazy Sale
- ❏ We'll Put Your Eggs in Two Baskets
- ❏ What Will You Do with the Extra Cash
- ❏ You'll Be Shocked at the Savings
- ❏ Zero In on Our Bargains

Promotions & Events
To Celebrate For April

- ❏ Alcohol Awareness Month
- ❏ Become a Yardbird Month
- ❏ Cancer Control Month
  Great Time to Discount Healthy Foods
- ❏ Couple Appreciation Month
  Buy One, Get One Free!
- ❏ Fresh Florida Tomatoes Month
- ❏ Grange Month
- ❏ Hans Christian Anderson Month
- ❏ Home Improvement Time
- ❏ Informed Women Month
- ❏ International Customer Loyalty Month
  What a great time to say "Thanks!"
- ❏ International Daffynitions Month
- ❏ International Legacy Month
- ❏ International Twit Award Month
- ❏ Keep America Beautiful Month
- ❏ Month of the Young Child
- ❏ Month of the Military Child
- ❏ National Car Care Month
  Automotive Accessorie Half Off!
- ❏ National Humor Month
- ❏ National Kite Month
- ❏ National Knuckle Down Month
- ❏ National Landscape Architecture Month
- ❏ National Lawn and Garden Month
  More Green in the Yard, More Green in Your Wallet
- ❏ National Pecan Month
- ❏ National Pet First Aid Awareness Month
- ❏ National Poetry Month
- ❏ National Soft Pretzel Month
- ❏ National Youth Sports Safety Month
- ❏ Physical Wellness Month
- ❏ Prevent Injuries America! Month

- ❏ Promise to Keep It Safe Prom Campaign
- ❏ School Library Media Month
- ❏ Soy Foods Month
- ❏ Sports Eye Safety Month
- ❏ Straw Hat Month
- ❏ Stress Awareness Month
- ❏ Southern Belles Month
  Y'all come in for a good deal, y'hear?
- ❏ Tackle Your Clutter Month
- ❏ Tour De Cure
- ❏ Women's Eye Health and Safety Month
- ❏ Boston Marathon
- ❏ The Masters Golf Championship
- ❏ NCAA Gymnastics Championship
- ❏ Pulitzer Prizes
- ❏ World Figure Skating Championship
- ❏ London Marathon
- ❏ Daylight Savings Time
- ❏ Kansas City Jazz Festival
- ❏ New Orleans Jazz Festival

Promotions & Events To Celebrate For April By Week

- ❏ Golden Rule Week . . . . April 1-7
- ❏ Laugh at Work Week . . . . April 1-7
- ❏ National Week of the Ocean . . . . April 3-9
  Our Prices Are Lower Than the Titanic!
- ❏ Week of the Young Child . . . . April 3-9
- ❏ National Blue Ribbon Week . . . . April 4-10
- ❏ National Garden Week . . . . April 10-16
- ❏ Electronic Communications Week . . . . April 10-16
- ❏ Astronomy Week . . . . April 11-17

APRIL

Promotions & Events
To Celebrate For April By Day

APRIL

❑ Kiss Your Mate Day . . . . April 28

❑ Arbor Day . . . . April 29
  Money Doesn't Grow on Trees…or Does It?

❑ Hairstylist Appreciation Day . . . . April 30

❑ Love Your Lawn Day . . . . April 30

❑ International Walk Day . . . . April 30

❑ National Honesty Day . . . . April 30
  We Cannot Tell a Lie…These Prices Are Insane!

Birthdays To Celebrate In April
(Can be used for either price or non price promotions)

❑ David Eisenhower . . . . April 1

❑ Anne McCaffrey. . . . . April 1

❑ Emmylou Harris . . . . April 2

❑ Hans Christian Andersen . . . . April 2

❑ Picabo Street . . . . April 3

❑ Eddie Murphy. . . . . April 3

❑ Maya Angelou . . . . April 4
  Birdcage Blowout!

❑ Russell Crowe. . . . . April 7

❑ Jackie Chan . . . . April 7

❑ Betty Ford . . . . April 8

❑ Hugh Hefner . . . . April 9

❑ Mandy Moore. . . . . April 10

- ❏ John Madden . . . . April 10
- ❏ Tom Clancy . . . . April 12
  * Make it a thriller of a sale*
- ❏ David Letterman . . . . April 12
- ❏ Pete Rose . . . . April 14
  Best Deal in Town – You Can Bet on It!
- ❏ Leonardo da Vinci . . . . April 15
- ❏ Conan O'Brien. . . . . April 18
- ❏ Hayden Christensen . . . . April 19
- ❏ Ashley Judd . . . . April 19
- ❏ Suge Knight. . . . . April 19
- ❏ Carmen Electra . . . . April 20
- ❏ Catherine The Great . . . . April 21
- ❏ Jack Nicholson . . . . April 22
  Best Jack Nicholson Impression Gets It Free!
- ❏ George Lopez . . . . April 23
- ❏ William Shakespeare. . . . . April 23
- ❏ Barbra Streisand . . . . April 24
- ❏ Al Pacino. . . . . April 25
- ❏ Jet Li . . . . April 26
- ❏ Casey Kasem . . . . April 27
- ❏ Jay Leno . . . . April 28
- ❏ Jerry Seinfeld . . . . April 29
- ❏ Michael Waltrip . . . . April 30

Need more dates? Check Out Chase's Calendar of Events!

NOTES

MAY

With Mother's Day, the Kentucky Derby, and Memorial Day Weekend in May, you might think you don't need any more promotional ideas. But you might want to give your customers something different: National Family Month is a great way to offer discounts for all ages, while Teacher Appreciation Days are awesome times to move apple-themed merchandise "out of season."

Classic May Sale Terms

- ❏ 21-Gun Salute Sales Event
- ❏ A Flag-Waving
- ❏ A Pearl of a Sale
- ❏ A Woman's Place Is at Our Sale
- ❏ Aaaaaaaaaaand They're Off
- ❏ After the Mint Juleps
- ❏ All-American
- ❏ All-American Memorial Weekend
- ❏ All-American Sale That's Out of the Blue
- ❏ As Good as Gold
- ❏ Because You Can
- ❏ Big Weekend, Small Prices

- ❏ Buy American and Save
- ❏ Buy Her Happiness
- ❏ Catch the Memorial Day Sale Wave
- ❏ Daily Double to Double Your Savings
- ❏ Democracy Appreciation
- ❏ Derby Dollar Days
- ❏ Doesn't Mom Deserve the Best
- ❏ Don't Forget Mother's Day!
- ❏ Down to the Wire
- ❏ Fill Your Cart and Save
- ❏ Fit for a Queen Queen for a Day

- ❏ Flag-Waving Savings
- ❏ For All She Does…
- ❏ For That Special Lady
- ❏ For the World's Best Mom
- ❏ For Your One in a Million Girl
- ❏ Freedom to Save More
- ❏ From the Heart
- ❏ Get What You Want
- ❏ Get What You Really Wanted
- ❏ Give Her the Best
- ❏ Granny Hour
- ❏ Great Grills for Less
  National Barbecue Month
- ❏ Guess What Mom Wants Most
- ❏ Hair Today, Gone Tomorrow
  Wig Promotion
  Don't Miss Cher's Birthday!
- ❏ Honor the Great Ones
- ❏ Honor Your Mother
- ❏ If You Can Say It, It's on Sale
- ❏ In Case You Forgot
- ❏ In Remembrance
- ❏ Is It Ever Enough?
- ❏ It's Better to Give, So Let Us!
- ❏ It's Derby Day Everyday
  at _____
- ❏ It's the Easiest Sale
  You'll Ever See
- ❏ Last Minute Gifts for Mom
- ❏ Leave Your Wallet at Home
- ❏ Luxuries for Mom!
  Savings for You!
- ❏ Make Her Friends Jealous
- ❏ Make It Up to Mom
- ❏ Make Mom's Wishes Come True
- ❏ Memorial Day Essentials:
  Family, Friends, Fun
- ❏ Memorial Day Extravaganza
- ❏ Memorial Day Parade of Values
- ❏ Memorial Day Weekend Sales
  Event
- ❏ Mum's the Word
- ❏ No Cure Beats a Manicure
- ❏ No More Excuses
- ❏ Open Late…She'll Never Know
  You Forgot
- ❏ Our Rugs Will Fly Forever.
  Our Sale Won't.
- ❏ Patriotic Duty to Save

MAY

- ❏ Post Time Is the Sale Time
- ❏ Pre-Mother's Day
- ❏ Pre-Season Sale
- ❏ Priced to Please
- ❏ Proud to Buy American
- ❏ Race Day
- ❏ Ready for Race Day
- ❏ Red, White, and Blue Sale
- ❏ Saddle Up with These Tremendous Deals
- ❏ Salute to Savings
- ❏ She Spoiled You... Now Spoil Her
- ❏ Show Her the Love
- ❏ Sneak Peek at Summer Savings
- ❏ Super Gifts for Super Moms
- ❏ Surprisingly Affordable
- ❏ Stop In In the Name of Love
- ❏ Straight Shootin'
- ❏ Take Her Breath Away
- ❏ Texas Hold-Em Draw and Save *World Series of Poker Events*
- ❏ Thank You Veterans!
- ❏ The Run for the Roses Event
- ❏ This Year You'll Remember
- ❏ Top Gift Ideas
- ❏ Trifecta Sale: Buy 3, Get 1 Free
- ❏ Triple Threat
- ❏ Triple Crown of Savings *Don't Forget the Kentucky Derby!*
- ❏ Yellow Ribbon
- ❏ We Remember
- ❏ We Won't Tell It Was on Sale
- ❏ We'll Bring the Bling Bling
- ❏ We're Selling Our Soles
- ❏ We've Got the Bling *Great for Liberace's Birthday!*
- ❏ What Do You Give the Most Special Person in the World?
- ❏ When Only the Finest Will Do
- ❏ Who's Your Mother's Day
- ❏ Win, Place, and Charge It!
- ❏ You'll Be Floored by Our Rugs *Bumpy Rug Day*
- ❏ You're Her Biggest Fan

Promotions & Events
To Celebrate For May

- Asian Pacific American Heritage Month
- Better Hearing and Speech Month
- Clean Air Month
- Creative Beginnings Month
- Family Support Month
- Family Wellness Month
- Get Caught Reading Month
- Haitian Heritage Month
- Heal the Children Month
- Healthy Vision Month
- Light the Night for Sight Month
- More Than Just a Pretty Face Month
- Motorcycle Safety Month
- National Barbeque Month
- National Bike Month
- National Correct Posture Month
- National Egg Month
- National Good Car Keeping Month
- National Hamburger Month
- National Mental Health Month
- National Military Appreciation Month
- National Moving Month
- National Physical Fitness & Sports Month
- National Salsa Month
- National Scholarship Month
- National Shoes for Orphans Month
- National Sight Saving Month
- National Revise Your Work Schedule Month
- Pilates Awareness Month
- Preparing Tomorrow's Parents Month
  Great for Baby Product Promotions
- Smiles Month
- Women's Health Care Month

- ☐ Young Achiever's Month
- ☐ National Family Month
  Buy One, Get Three Free!

- ☐ Indianapolis 500
- ☐ Kentucky Derby

Promotions & Events
To Celebrate For May By Week

- ☐ National Read for Leisure Week . . . . May 1-7
- ☐ Goodwill Industries Week . . . . May 1-7
- ☐ Pen Friends Week . . . . May 1-7
- ☐ Take a Smart Risk Week . . . . May 1-7
- ☐ National Peace of Mind Week . . . . May 1-7
  All Security Systems on Sale!
- ☐ Be Kind to Animals Week . . . . May 1-7
- ☐ Flexible Work Arrangement Week . . . . May 1-7
- ☐ National Family Week . . . . May 1-7
- ☐ National PTA Teacher's Appreciation . . . . May 1-7
- ☐ National Hug Holiday Week . . . . May 1-7
- ☐ National Pet Week . . . . May 1-7
- ☐ National Postcard Week . . . . May 1-7
- ☐ Teacher Appreciation Week . . . . May 1-7
  Have an Apple Themed Promotion
- ☐ Update Your References Week . . . . May 2-6
- ☐ National Wildflower Week . . . . May 2-8
- ☐ National Historic Preservation Week . . . . May 2-8
  Today's Things at Yesterday's Prices

National Police Week

Prices so low they should be against the law!

MAY

Promotions & Events
To Celebrate For May By Day

❑ Executive Coaching Day . . . . May 1

❑ Frequent Flyer Day . . . . May 1

❑ Law Day . . . . May 1

❑ Loyalty Day . . . . May 1
  Regular Customers Save More!

❑ May Day . . . . May 1

❑ Mother Goose Day . . . . May 1

❑ Soil Stewardship Day . . . . May 1

❑ Save the Rhino Day. . . . . May 1

❑ School Principals Day . . . . May 1

❑ Stepmother's Day. . . . . May 1

❑ Robert's Rules of Order Day . . . . May 2

❑ Sibling Appreciation Day . . . . May 2

❑ National Teacher Day. . . . . May 3

❑ Pregnancy Fitness Awareness Day . . . . May 3

❑ Lumpy Rug Day. . . . . May 3

❑ Paranormal Day . . . . May 3
  Our Deals Are Out of This World!

❑ Wordsmith Day. . . . . May 3

❑ World Press Freedom Day . . . . May 3

❑ Relationship Renewal Day . . . . May 4

❑ Kite Day . . . . May 4

MAY

MAY

Best Sale and Promotional Ideas by Month   143

- ❑ Find Your Soul Mate Day. . . . . .May 22
- ❑ National Maritime Day . . . . .May 22
- ❑ Neighbor Day . . . . .May 22
- ❑ World Turtle Day . . . . .May 23
- ❑ Brother's Day . . . . .May 24
- ❑ National Tap Dance Day . . . . .May 25
- ❑ Great American Grump Out Day . . . . .May 25
- ❑ National Senior Health & Fitness Day . . . . .May 25
- ❑ Morning Radio Wise Guy Day . . . . .May 28
- ❑ International Jazz Day . . . . .May 28
- ❑ Ancestor Honor Day . . . . .May 30
- ❑ Memorial Day. . . . . May 30
- ❑ Loomis Day . . . . .May 30
- ❑ What You Think Upon Grows Day . . . . .May 31

Birthdays To Celebrate In May
(Can be used for either price or non price promotions)

- ❑ Tim McGraw. . . . . May 1
- ❑ David Beckham. . . . . May 2
- ❑ Dwayne "The Rock" Johnson . . . . May 2
- ❑ James Brown . . . . May 3
- ❑ Greg Gumbel . . . . May 3
- ❑ Brian Williams . . . . May 5

MAY

❏ Al Franken . . . . .May 21

❏ Naomi Campbell . . . . .May 22

❏ Sir Arthur Conan Doyle . . . . .May 22
   Great for Sherlock Holmes Promo!

❏ Jewel . . . . .May 23

❏ Drew Carey . . . . .May 23

❏ Bob Dylan . . . . .May 24

❏ Tommy Chong . . . . .May 24
   Watch for the Tie-Dyed Tags!

❏ Lauryn Hill . . . . .May 25

❏ Mike Myers . . . . .May 25

❏ Lenny Kravitz . . . . .May 26

❏ Hank Williams, Jr. . . . . .May 26

❏ John Wayne . . . . .May 26

❏ Lisa "Left Eye" Lopes . . . . .May 27

❏ Wild Bill Hickok . . . . .May 27

❏ Jamie Oliver . . . . .May 27

❏ Melissa Etheridge . . . . .May 29

❏ Wynonna Judd . . . . .May 30

❏ Mel Blanc . . . . .May 30

❏ Clint Eastwood . . . . .May 31
   Let Us Make Your Day!

**Chase's Calendar of Events has even more
events, festivals and celebrations!**

NOTES

MAY

JUNE

For a month where nothing 'happens', there's sure a lot to promo in June. Father's Day is the lone holiday, but with high school and college graduations, golf, fishing, and tennis all in high gear, and of course, the drama that is Hug Your Cat Day, there's never a dull moment!

Classic June Sale Terms

- ❑ A Once-In-A-Lifetime-Hole-In-One Sale Event
- ❑ Add Zing to Your Swing
- ❑ After Father's Day Sale
- ❑ Attention: Golf Addicts!
- ❑ Beat the Pro Sales Event
- ❑ Boys of Summer
- ❑ Boys Toys
- ❑ Boys Will Be Boys
- ❑ Buy All You Want, We'll Make More
- ❑ Capture the Memory
- ❑ Capture the Moment
- ❑ Caught You Looking
- ❑ Celebrate Summer

- ❑ C'mon, You Know What Dad Wants
- ❑ Congratulations Class of _____
- ❑ Country Fair
- ❑ Country Jamboree
- ❑ Dad's Day
- ❑ Don't Tee Me Off Sales Event
- ❑ Dress Up Dad
- ❑ Doesn't Dad Deserve the Best?
- ❑ Don't Forget Dad!
- ❑ Family Fun in the Sun...for Less
- ❑ Fathers Only Sales Event
- ❑ Fill the Pail
- ❑ Firecracker Sale

- ❏ Fish Out Your Discount
- ❏ Fit for a King
- ❏ For the World's Greatest Dad
- ❏ Golf Sale for Dad
- ❏ Grab a Cold One
- ❏ Graduation Party Headquarters
- ❏ Great Deals for Great Dads
- ❏ Happy Days Are Here Again
- ❏ Hit the Beach
- ❏ Hooked on Our Fish
- ❏ Ice Cold
- ❏ I'd Rather Be Golfing Sales Event
- ❏ If It's in the Rainbow, It's Reduced
- ❏ If You Can't Stand the Heat – Come on In!
- ❏ It's Okay to Play
- ❏ It's Tick Season, Do You Have Your Clock with You?
- ❏ June Is for Junipers – and the Rest of Our Trees
- ❏ Just in Time for Father's Day
- ❏ Ka-boom! Summer Blast Off
- ❏ Miles of Smiles
- ❏ Nothing Says Summer Like Our Hot Sale
- ❏ Only Our Lures Are Fishy
- ❏ Our Fishing Sale Is Gonna Getcha
- ❏ Outdoor Living Sale
- ❏ Peek at Our Summer Savings
- ❏ Pirate's Booty Sale *johnny Depp's Birthday!*
- ❏ Pomp and Circumstance
- ❏ Quarterly _____
- ❏ Saluting America's Dads
- ❏ Scuba Dooba Done
- ❏ Semi-Annual Sale
- ❏ Sensational Summer
- ❏ Shell Out Fewer Clams – Beach Sale
- ❏ Shore Thing
- ❏ Short Short Shorts Sale
- ❏ Spoil Him Rotten
- ❏ Start Your Engines
- ❏ State of the Art Stuff

- ❏ Stop Wishing
- ❏ Summer Blast Off Sale
- ❏ Summer Camp Stock Up
- ❏ Summer Safari
- ❏ Summer Sale Goes Out in a Blaze of Glory
- ❏ Summer Shape-Up
- ❏ Summer Solstice
- ❏ Summer Sundays
- ❏ Summerfest
- ❏ Summerswap
- ❏ Sunday Sun Splash
- ❏ Sunrise to Sunset
- ❏ Sunny Sunday
- ❏ Sun-Sational
- ❏ Sunset Savings
- ❏ Super Summer
- ❏ Super Summer Coupon
- ❏ Surf, Print, and Save
- ❏ The Best Is Yet to Come: Gifts for Your Grad
- ❏ The Grand Slam Golf Sale
- ❏ The Summer of Our Content
- ❏ The Tassel Is Worth the Hassle Sales Event

- ❏ There's Nothing Fishy Here *Take a Kid Fishing Weekend*
- ❏ Top Ten Most Wanted... Father's Day Gifts
- ❏ Tourist Appreciation
- ❏ Vacation Goods
- ❏ Watch Out World! Here Comes the Class Of _____
- ❏ Weekend Wackiness
- ❏ Weekend Warrior
- ❏ Wet and Wild Sale
- ❏ Whale of a Sale
- ❏ What a Summer
- ❏ What He Really Wants
- ❏ When Only the Finest Will Do
- ❏ Who's Your Father's Day
- ❏ X Marks the Sale

Promotions & Events
To Celebrate For June

- Adopt a Shelter Cat Month
- Cancer From the Sun Month
  Buy a Floppy Hat, Get the Sunscreen Free!
- Celibacy Awareness Month
- Child Vision Awareness Month
- Effective Communications Month
- Fireworks Safety Month
- Gay and Lesbian Pride Month
- International Men's Month
- Dairy Month
  There's nothing cheesy about our sale!
- No Dairy Month
- June Is Lane Courtesy Month
- June Is Perennial Gardening Month
- June Is Turkey Lover's Month
- National Accordion Awareness Month
- National Candy Month
  Come in for Sweet Savings
- National Gay, Lesbian, Bisexual, & Transgender Month
- National Ice Tea Month
- National Rivers Month
- National Rose Month
- National Safety Month
- National Soul Food Month
- Potty Training Awareness Month
  Come to Our Flood Sale
- Professional Wellness Month
- Rebuild Your Life Month
- Sports America Kids Month
- Student Safety Month
- Vision Research Month
- College World Series
- Backgammon World Championships
- Us Open
- Nba Championship
- Stanley Cup
- Ncaa Women's Softball World Series
- Wimbledon

Promotions & Events
To Celebrate For June By Week

- ❑ International Volunteers Week . . . . .June 1-7
- ❑ Stepparents Week . . . . .June 1-7
- ❑ Black Single Parents Week . . . . June 5-11
- ❑ Superman Week . . . . June 9-12
- ❑ Take a Kid Fishing Weekend. . . . . June 10-12
- ❑ National Flag Week . . . . June 12-18
- ❑ National Hermit Week . . . . June 13-20
  Even a Hermit Can't Resist!
- ❑ Families in Business Week . . . . June 13-17
- ❑ Meet a Mate Week . . . . June 13-19
- ❑ National Little League Baseball Week . . . . June 13-19
- ❑ Dick Tracy Days . . . . June 15-19
- ❑ Universal Father's Week . . . . June 19-25
- ❑ Carpenter Ant Awareness Week . . . . June 19-25
  Really Small Hammers Half Off!
- ❑ Watermelon Thump Week . . . . June 23-26

Promotions & Events
To Celebrate For June By Day

❏ National Tailors Day . . . . June 1

❏ Leave the Office Early Day . . . . June 2
Sales Event Starts at 3 PM!

❏ National Bubba Day . . . . June 2

❏ Chimborazo Day . . . . June 3
Celebrates a Mountain in Ecuador

❏ Hug Your Cat Day . . . . June 3

❏ Dog Appreciation Day . . . . June 3

❏ Give Your Dog a Bone Day . . . . June 4
Who Says It's a Dog's Life?

❏ Apple Computer Day . . . . June 4

❏ Cheer Coach Day . . . . June 4

❏ National Trails Day . . . . June 4

❏ AIDS Day . . . . June 5

❏ World Environment Day . . . . June 5

❏ National Cancer Survivors Day . . . . June 5

❏ D Day Commemoration . . . . June 6

❏ Upsy Daisy Day . . . . June 8

❏ Wicket World of Croquet Day . . . . June 11

❏ Children's Sunday . . . . June 12

❏ Crowded Nest Awareness Day . . . . June 12

JUNE

- [ ] Decide to Be Married Day . . . . June 27

- [ ] "Happy Birthday to You" Day . . . . June 27

- [ ] Helen Keller Day . . . . June 27

- [ ] Please Take My Children to Work Day . . . . June 27

- [ ] Hand Shake Day . . . . June 28

- [ ] National Columnists Day . . . . June 28
  Bring in your favorite newspaper column for 10% off!

- [ ] Leap Second Time Adjustment Day . . . . June 30

Birthdays To Celebrate In June
(Can be used for either price or non price promotions)

- [ ] Marilyn Monroe . . . . June 1

- [ ] Wayne Brady . . . . June 2

- [ ] Angelina Jolie. . . . . June 4

- [ ] Dr. Ruth Westheimer. . . . . June 4

- [ ] Brian McKnight. . . . . June 5

- [ ] Anna Kournikova . . . . June 7

- [ ] Kanye West . . . . June 8

- [ ] Joan Rivers . . . . June 8
  Lasts Forever and Cheap!

- [ ] Barbara Bush . . . . June 8

- [ ] Natalie Portman . . . . June 9

- [ ] Johnny Depp . . . . June 9
  Pirate Promotions

**Need more dates? Check Out
Chase's Calendar of Events!**

NOTES

JUNE

JULY

Patriotic promotions celebrating Independence Day dominate July, as do campaigns centering on summer sun and fun. Other lesser known yet still profitable options remain, including National Hot Dog Month – Come to Our Sidewalk BBQ Sale! – or Embrace Your Geekness Day, when Palm Pilots, Laptops, and Gaming Systems move like hotcakes!

Classic July Sale Terms

- ❏ 4th of July Celebration
- ❏ 4th of July Hot Buys
- ❏ 4th of July Marathon Sale
- ❏ 4th of July Specials
- ❏ A Flag Waving Sale
- ❏ Add a Shot of Sunshine
- ❏ All American Sale
- ❏ All American Savings
- ❏ A Real Summer Treat
- ❏ Beach Blast
- ❏ Biggest Barbecue of the Year
- ❏ Blazin' Summer Savin'
- ❏ Come In, Cool Off, and Save!
- ❏ Cook Up a Colorful Celebration
- ❏ Declaration of Savings
- ❏ Declare Independence From High Prices!
- ❏ Don't Forget the Sunscreen!
- ❏ Don't Let the Parade Pass You By
- ❏ Dynamite Offers for the 4th
- ❏ Explosive 4th of July Savings
- ❏ Extended Summer Hours
- ❏ Festival of Freedom
- ❏ Fill the Cooler for Less
- ❏ Firecracker Sale
- ❏ Fireworks Sale Extravaganza
- ❏ Flag Waving Savings
- ❏ Food! Fun! Fireworks!

- ❏ Fourth of July Sale Blowout!
- ❏ From Sunscreen to Ice cream
- ❏ Fun in the Sun
- ❏ Happy Birthday America!
- ❏ Happy Fourth of July Specials
- ❏ Hot! Hot! Hot! Sizzling Summer Savings!
- ❏ Hottest Sale of the Summer
- ❏ It's a Yankee Doodle Dandy of a Deal!
- ❏ Join Our "Fan Club"
- ❏ Knock Off Early
- ❏ Last Minute Party Supply Station
- ❏ Life, Liberty, and the Pursuit of a Cookout
- ❏ Live the Good Life
- ❏ Made in the USA
- ❏ More Bang for Your Buck!
- ❏ More for Less
- ❏ Old Fashioned Prices
- ❏ One Hour Only!
- ❏ Our Biggest Fans
- ❏ Outta Sight Saturday
- ❏ Parade of Values

- ❏ Pick a Pair for Less
- ❏ Prepare to Be Amazed
- ❏ Race Day Bargain
- ❏ Ready, Aim, Fire Up the Savings
- ❏ Safari of Savings
- ❏ Saturday Savings All Summer Long
- ❏ Save Often, Save Early
- ❏ Sensational Summer Sale
- ❏ Share Our Air (Conditioning)
- ❏ Shell Out Fewer Clams – Beach Sale
- ❏ Shore Thing
- ❏ Short Short Shorts Sale
- ❏ Show Us Your True Colors
- ❏ Soar Into Savings
- ❏ Sparkling July Summer
- ❏ Star Spangled Savings
- ❏ Steak Your Claim on Grilles
- ❏ Stock the Fridge
- ❏ Stock Up on 4th of July Barbecues
- ❏ Summer Safari
- ❏ Summer Sundays Mean Savings
- ❏ Summer Survival Kit

- SummerFest
- Summerswap
- Super Summer
- Super Summer Coupon
- Sunday Sun Splash
- Sunny Sunday
- Swim Into Sweet Deals
- Take It From Us
- Temperatures Go Up, Prices Go Down
- These Are the Days
- Think You Can Pass Up a Sale This Great?
- The More You Buy, The More You Save
- The Summer of Our Content
- Three Cheers for the Red, White, and Blue
- To Go or Not to Go, That Is the Question

- Tourist Appreciation
- Treat the Family
- Treat Yourself
- Wacky Weekend
- We All Scream for Ice Cream
- We Salute You with Our July Savings
- Wear Your Uniform and Save
- Weekend Warriors Pay Less!
- We're Showing Our True Colors: Red, White, and Blue!
- We've Got the Spirit
- What a Summer!
- What You Want Is on Sale
- Wild Weekend
- You Win When _____ Wins!
- You'll Love It

Promotions & Events
To Celebrate For July

- ❏ Anti-Boredom Month
- ❏ Cell Phone Courtesy Month
- ❏ Herbal/Prescription Awareness Month
- ❏ International Blondie/ Deborah Harry Month
- ❏ National Baked Beans Month
- ❏ National Doghouse Repairs Month
- ❏ National Hot Dog Month
- ❏ Blueberries Month
- ❏ National Purposeful Parenting Month
- ❏ National Recreation and Parks Month
- ❏ National Water Gardening Month
- ❏ Roots and Branches Month
- ❏ Social Wellness Month
- ❏ Women's Motorcycle Month
- ❏ Tour de France
- ❏ NASCAR's Pepsi 400
- ❏ British Grand Prix
- ❏ The British Open Championship
- ❏ Calgary Stampede
- ❏ Wimbledon
- ❏ Midnight Sun Marathon
- ❏ The Baja 500

Promotions & Events
To Celebrate For July By Week

- ❏ National Education Association Week . . . . July 1-6
- ❏ National Unassisted Homebirth Week. . . . . July 1-7
  Buy six towels, we'll throw in the hot water for free!
- ❏ Special Recreation Week . . . . July 3-9
- ❏ Freedom from Fear of Speaking Week . . . . July 3-9
- ❏ Be Nice to New Jersey Week . . . . July 3-9

❑ Barbershop Quartet Singing Week . . . . July 3-9

❑ Air Conditioning Appreciation Week . . . . July 3-9

❑ Freedom Week . . . . July 3-9

❑ Take Charge of Change Week . . . . .July 10-16

❑ National Farriers Week . . . . .July 10-16

❑ Rabbit Week . . . . .July 15-21
    Buy Two Rabbits, Get More Free!

❑ National Salad Week . . . . .July 25-31

Promotions & Events
To Celebrate For July By Day

❑ I Forgot Day . . . . .July 2

❑ Air Conditioning Appreciation Day . . . . .July 3
    Cool Prices on Hot Products!

❑ Compliment Your Mirror Day .July 3

❑ Stay Out of the Sun Day . . . . .July 3

❑ Independence Day . . . . .July 4

❑ Independence From Meat Day . . . . .July 4

❑ Take Your Webmaster to Lunch Day . . . . .July 6

❑ Father/Daughter Take a Walk Together Day . . . . .July 7

❑ Clerihew Day . . . . .July 10

❑ Don't Step on a Bee Day . . . . .July 10
    Epi-Pens and Bandaid Discounts Storewide!

❑ World Population Day . . . . .July 11

❑ Embrace Your Geekness Day . . . . .July 13
    High Tech Half Off!

❏ Gruntled Workers Day . . . . July 13

❏ Be a Dork Day . . . . July 15

❏ Zippo Day . . . . July 16

❏ Cow Appreciation Day . . . . July 16

❏ Shark Awareness Day . . . . July 16

❏ Woodie Wagon Day . . . . July 16

❏ National Ice Cream Day . . . . July 17
Come in for a Free Cone!

❏ National Get Out of the Doghouse Day . . . . July 18

❏ Moon Day . . . . July 20

❏ Get to Know Your Customers Day . . . . July 21

❏ Gorgeous Grandma Day . . . . July 23
Enter Our Gorgeous Grandma Contest!

❏ Hot Enough For Ya Day . . . . July 23

❏ Cousins Day . . . . July 24

❏ Virtual Love Day . . . . July 24

❏ Parents' Day . . . . July 24

❏ Day Out of Time Day . . . . July 25

❏ Take Your Houseplant for a Walk Day . . . . July 27

❏ Walk on Stilts Day . . . . July 27
All Top Shelf Items Discounted!

❏ National Drive Thru Day . . . . July 28

❏ All-American Soap Box Derby Day . . . . July 31

❏ Mutt's Day . . . . July 31

Birthdays To Celebrate In July
(Can be used for either price or non price promotions)

- ❏ Liv Tyler . . . . .July 1
- ❏ Missy Elliott . . . . .July 1
- ❏ Pamela Anderson . . . . .July 1
- ❏ Deborah Harry . . . . .July 1
- ❏ Lindsay Lohan . . . . .July 2
- ❏ Jose Canseco . . . . .July 2
- ❏ Tom Cruise. . . . . .July 3
- ❏ Franz Kafka . . . . .July 3
  We're Bugging Out of Here!
- ❏ Montel Williams . . . . .July 3
- ❏ Geraldo Rivera . . . . .July 4
- ❏ PT Barnum . . . . .July 5
  Great for Circus Themed Promotions
- ❏ 50 Cent . . . . .July 6
- ❏ George W. Bush . . . . .July 6
- ❏ Dalai Lama . . . . .July 6
- ❏ Nancy Reagan . . . . .July 6
- ❏ Ringo Starr . . . . .July 7
- ❏ Toby Keith. . . . . .July 8
- ❏ Marianne Williamson .July 8
- ❏ Courtney Love. . . . . .July 9
- ❏ Tom Hanks . . . . .July 9

❏ John Tesh . . . . July 9

❏ Jessica Simpson . . . . July 10

❏ Richard Simmons. . . . . July 12

❏ Bill Cosby . . . . July 12

❏ Cheech Marin . . . . July 13

❏ Harrison Ford . . . . July 13

❏ Patrick Stewart . . . . July 13

❏ Gerald Ford . . . . July 14

❏ Carlos Santana . . . . July 20

❏ Robin Williams . . . . July 21

❏ Ernest Hemingway . . . . July 21

❏ Don Knotts . . . . July 21

❏ Albert Brooks . . . . July 22

❏ Alex Trebek . . . . July 22
I'll take low prices for $500, Alex!

❏ Don Imus . . . . July 23

❏ Jennifer Lopez . . . . July 24

❏ Carl Jung. . . . . July 26

❏ Beatrix Potter . . . . July 28
Peter Rabbit Merchandise on Sale!

❏ Arnold Schwarzenegger. . . . . July 30

❏ JK Rowling . . . . July 31
Hogwild for Hogwarts: Magic Harry Potter Sale!

Need More Dates? Check Out Chase's Calendar of Events!

NOTES

AUGUST

Did you think nothing happened in August? Everyone else thought so too – which is why lots and lots of lesser known holidays are crammed into one short month. Newspaper reporters call the end of August "The Silly Season", so don't be afraid to try a funny promotion – you'll likely get some press. From Lefthander's Day to that perennial classic "Sneak Some Zucchini Onto Your Neighbor's Porch" festivities, you're sure to find a day worth celebrating! Add in the beginning of Back to School season, and you'll have non-stop sales!

Classic August Sale Terms

- ❑ A 9-Inning Sale
  Little League World Series
- ❑ Back to School
- ❑ Back to School Bargains
- ❑ Back to School Blowout
- ❑ Back to School Bonanza
- ❑ Back to School for Less
- ❑ Bring on the Season
- ❑ Celebrate Summer
- ❑ Classes Start Soon!
- ❑ Decorate the Dorm for Less
- ❑ Dog Days

- ❑ Dogs Eat Free
- ❑ Doggone Great
- ❑ Dorm Daze
- ❑ Dorm Delights
- ❑ Dress for Success
- ❑ Early Bird Specials
- ❑ End of Season BBQ Blowout
- ❑ Everything for Back to School
- ❑ Everything You Need for Less
- ❑ Fall's Right Around the Corner
- ❑ Family _____ Sale
- ❑ Fat Wallet Sale

- ❑ Get Ready for Back to School
- ❑ Get the Look You Like
- ❑ Get Your Gift for Your Juliet Yet?
  Girlfriends Day
- ❑ Gimme a Back-To-School
- ❑ Good Things Come to Those Who Wait – Seasonal Merchandise Clearance
- ❑ Gotta Get It Sale
- ❑ Hard Bargains on Software
- ❑ Hit the Beach
- ❑ If You Can Spell It It's on Sale
- ❑ If You Can't Stand the Heat – Come on In
- ❑ It's the Best Back-To-School Sale in Its Class
- ❑ It's What's Next
- ❑ Kick Off the Season with Our
- ❑ King Sale
  Great for Elvis Themed Promotions
- ❑ Last Blast
- ❑ Layaway for Later
- ❑ Lefties Pay Less

- ❑ Lefty Days
  International Lefthander's Day
- ❑ Listen to Your Kids
- ❑ Love Lasts Forever, but This Sale Won't
- ❑ Martha's Favorite
  Martha Stewart's Birthday
- ❑ Money Talks Louder Than Usual
- ❑ More Bang for Your Back to School Buck
- ❑ New Merchandise
- ❑ Nothing Says Summer Like Our Hot Sale
- ❑ Nothing to Sneeze at Sale
- ❑ Our Back to School Extravaganza Begins Now
- ❑ Outfit Your Family for Less
- ❑ Pick a Pair
- ❑ Pre-Season
- ❑ Remember September
- ❑ Rev Up for Shopping Season
- ❑ Same Look for Less: Back to School Fashion
- ❑ School Days
- ❑ School Daze

- ❏ Seasonal Merchandise Marked Way Down
- ❏ See for Yourself
- ❏ Seize the August Days Sales Event
- ❏ Sensational Summer
- ❏ September's Coming!
- ❏ Seriously Fun Shopping
- ❏ Shop Early and Save
- ❏ Short Short Shorts Sale
- ❏ Show Her You Love Her
- ❏ Sizzlin' Summer Sale
- ❏ Slip Into Fall
- ❏ Smart Start for the School Year
- ❏ Soar Into Savings *National Aviation Week*
- ❏ Spoil Her Rotten
- ❏ Start Saving Sooner

- ❏ Start the New Year Right
- ❏ Store Your Stuff
- ❏ Student Discount
- ❏ Summer Sale Goes Out in a Blaze of Glory
- ❏ Super Autumn Values Available Now
- ❏ Super Summer
- ❏ Support the Right to Armchairs
- ❏ Sweetheart of a
- ❏ The Last Best Sale of the Season
- ❏ The Sales Are Under There! Underwear? *National Underwear Day*
- ❏ The Way to a Woman's Heart Is Through Her Jewelry *Great for Girlfriend's Day*
- ❏ This One Was Made Just for You
- ❏ Twist Our Arm
- ❏ Update Your Wardrobe

Dog Days PRICE FREEZE

- We Know What You Need for Back to School
- Welcome Students
- What Your Kids Want
- Who Let the Dogs Out: Dog Days of Summer Sellabration
- Will It Ever End Beach Blowout
- Womyn Only
- What a Summer

- What Would Martha Buy? *Martha Stewart's Birthday*
- What Would Martha Save? *Martha Stewart's Birthday*
- WWMD (What Would Martha Do?) *Martha Stewart's Birthday*
- You Can Have Them All
- You'll Be Spoiled by Our Fresh Pricing
- Your Wallet Will Thank You

Promotions & Events To Celebrate For August

- Black Business Month
- Children's Eye Health and Safety Month
- Children's Vision & Learning Month
- Happiness Happens Month
- May Your Reading Be a Haven Month
- National Inventor's Month
- National Toddler's Month *Super Mega Toy Sale!*

- National Win with Civility Month
- Video Music Awards
- Little League World Series
- PGA Championship
- US Open
- Highland Games
- Georgia Shakespeare Festival
- Burning Man Festival

Promotions & Events
To Celebrate For August By Week

- ❏ Simplify Your Life Week . . . . August 1-7
- ❏ World Breastfeeding Week . . . . August 1-7
- ❏ Psychic Week . . . . August 1-5
- ❏ Knights of Columbus Family Week . . . . .August 6-14
- ❏ National Scrabble Week .August 7-12
  Spell Out the Savings!
- ❏ Don't Wait! Celebrate Week . . . . .August 8-14
- ❏ Elvis Week . . . . .August 8-14
  King Sized Bargains
- ❏ Kool-Aid Days . . . . August 12-14
- ❏ National Resurrect Romance Week . . . . August 14-20
  Hot Days, Hotter Nights
- ❏ Thanks for All the Gifts Week . . . . August 14-20
- ❏ Weird Contest Week . . . . August 15-21
  Hold a Silly Competition
- ❏ National Aviation Week . . . . August 16-22
  Soar into Savings
- ❏ Be Kind to Humankind Week . . . . August 25-31

Promotions & Events
To Celebrate For August By Day

❑ Braham Pie Day . . . . .August 1

❑ Girlfriend's Day . . . . .August 1
  Show Her How Much You Care!

❑ Respect for Parent's Day .August 1

❑ Rounds Resounding Day. .August 1

❑ National Night Out . . . . .August 2

❑ National Pretty Is as Pretty Does Day . . . . .August 2

❑ Friendship Day . . . . .August 3
  BOGO

❑ Coast Guard Day . . . . .August 4

❑ Work Like a Dog Day . . . . .August 5

❑ National Fresh Breath Day. . . . . .August 6

❑ National Mustard Day . . . . .August 6
  All Yellow Tag Items 25% Off!

❑ Women's Pro Football Day. . . . . .August 6

❑ Particularly Preposterous Packaging Day . . . . .August 7

❑ National Kid's Day . . . . .August 7

❑ Sister's Day . . . . .August 7

❑ Treasure Your Customers Day . . . . .August 7

❑ The Date to Create Day . . . . .August 8
  Art and Craft Promotion

❑ Happiness Happens Day . . . . .August 8

Rootbeer Float Day

Birthdays To Celebrate In August
(Can be used for either price or non price promotions)

- Jerry Garcia . . . . .August 1
- Yves Saint Laurent . . . . .August 1
  YSL Promotions Galore
- Martha Stewart. . . . . .August 3
  What Would Martha Buy?
- Jeff Gordon . . . . .August 4
- Barack Obama . . . . .August 4
- Neil Armstrong . . . . .August 5
  These Deals Are Out of This World!
- Garrison Keillor . . . . .August 7
- Dustin Hoffman. . . . . .August 8
- Whitney Houston . . . . .August 9
- Jimmy Dean . . . . August 10
  Save on Sausage!
- George Hamilton . . . . August 12
  If It's Tan, It's on Sale!
- Alfred Hitchcock . . . . August 13
- Halle Berry . . . . August 14
- Steve Martin . . . . August 14
- Lynne Cheney . . . . August 14
- Julia Child . . . . August 15
  Fine Cookware Fiesta!

❏ Madonna . . . . August 16

❏ Robert de Niro . . . . August 17

❏ Robert Redford . . . . August 18

❏ Bill Clinton . . . . August 19

❏ Gene Roddenberry . . . . August 19
One Day Only Star Trek Extravaganza!

❏ Ray Bradbury . . . . August 22
451 Items on Sale Inside!

❏ Marlee Matlin . . . . August 24

❏ Monty Hall . . . . August 25

❏ Rachel Ray . . . . August 25

❏ Tim Burton . . . . August 25

❏ Regis Philbin . . . . August 25

❏ Robin Leach . . . . August 29

Need more information on these dates?
Check Out Chase's Calendar of Events!

NOTES

SEPTEMBER

Your customers are expecting Back To School and Labor Day promotions as soon as the leaves start falling. Give them that and more, with unusual sales opportunities like Fortune Cookie Day and Bald Is Beautiful Day. How many men could you draw in with a "Show Us Your Sexy Chrome Dome" Contest?

Classic September Sale Terms

- ❑ A Little Knowledge Is a Dangerous Thing, But This Sale Isn't
- ❑ A Mind-Expanding Back to School
- ❑ A Very Special Sale That's ... Top Secret
- ❑ Amazing Savings
- ❑ Amazing Summer's End
- ❑ At The Head of the Class
- ❑ Autumn Color Accents
- ❑ Back 2 School
- ❑ Back at Class... Everything's Now On
- ❑ Back at School
- ❑ Back to Basics

- ❑ Back to School
- ❑ Back to School Kick-Off
- ❑ Back to the Dorm
- ❑ Be the One They Envy
- ❑ Be Your Own Role Model
- ❑ Best of Fall
- ❑ Best Selling Fashions for Less
- ❑ Brand Name
- ❑ Bring on the Savings
- ❑ Bring Them Home
- ❑ Children's Hour
- ❑ Clean Out Your Closet
- ❑ Cushion Your Fall – Luxury Pillow Sale
- ❑ Don't Blame Us if You Miss It

- ❏ Door Buster Sale
- ❏ Dorm Daze
- ❏ Dress for Success
- ❏ Everything You Need for School
- ❏ Fall Clean-Up
- ❏ Fall Colors
- ❏ Fall Family Fest
- ❏ Fall Fashion Week
- ❏ Fall Fest
- ❏ Fall Festival
- ❏ Fall Festival of Leaves
- ❏ Fall Fiesta
- ❏ Fall Furniture Extravaganza
- ❏ Fall Home Festival
- ❏ Fall in Love All Over Again
- ❏ Fall Into a Great
- ❏ Fall Into Fashion
- ❏ Fall Into Our
- ❏ Fall Kickoff
- ❏ Fall Lawn and Garden
- ❏ Fall Starts Here…with Our Super Fall Sale

- ❏ Fall Stock-Up Selection
- ❏ Falling Leaves, Falling Prices
- ❏ Focus on Saving More
- ❏ Fortune Cookie Freebies *Fortune Cookie Day*
- ❏ Fortune's Smiling on You *Fortune Cookie Day*
- ❏ Get the Look You Like
- ❏ Gimme a Back-To-School
- ❏ Great Minds Shop Here
- ❏ Happy Days Are Here Again
- ❏ Highest Quality, Cheapest Prices
- ❏ If You Can Read This, You're Close Enough to Be Saving Money
- ❏ In Remembrance *POW/MIA Remembrance Day*
- ❏ Invest in Yourself
- ❏ It Is Rocket Science – Text Book Sale
- ❏ It's Our Big Labor Day Sale
- ❏ It's the Best Back-To-School Sale in Its Class
- ❏ Kick Off the Season
- ❏ Labor Day Extravaganza
- ❏ Labor Day Summer Clearance

- ❑ Labor Day Weekend
- ❑ Last Minute School Supplies
- ❑ Last Week of Summer
- ❑ Lawaway for Later
- ❑ Leaf the Discounts to the Pros
- ❑ Listen to Your Kids
- ❑ More Bags for Your Buck
- ❑ New Start Sale
- ❑ Online Coupons
- ❑ Open Labor Day
- ❑ Open Labor Day for This
- ❑ Our Back to School Sale Continues
- ❑ Pre-Labor Day Specials
- ❑ Prices Are Falling with the Leaves
- ❑ Quarterly Super Sale
- ❑ Same Look for Less
- ❑ Save a Bundle Sale
- ❑ School Days
- ❑ School Daze
- ❑ Secret Coupon Sale
- ❑ September Is for Students

- ❑ Sew Up Your Bargains
- ❑ Shop Til You Drop Sale
- ❑ Show Your School ID and Save
- ❑ Slip Into Fall
- ❑ Spectacular Autumn
- ❑ Stock Up on School Supplies
- ❑ Student Appreciation
- ❑ Student Discount
- ❑ Super Autumn Values Are Now On
- ❑ Super Labor Day Sale
- ❑ The Look for Less
- ❑ The Sale You've Been Waiting For
- ❑ This Year's Fashions at Last Year's Prices

Promotions & Events
To Celebrate For September

❑ Baby Safety Month

❑ Backpack Safety America Month

❑ Be Kind to Editors and Writers Month
Buy 2 Books, Get One Free!

❑ Children's Good Manners Month

❑ College Savings Month

❑ Fall Hat Month
Enter Our Wacky Hat Contest!

❑ California Wild Rice Month

❑ Hug a Texas Chef Month

❑ International Gay Square Dancing Month

❑ International People Skills Month

❑ International Self-Awareness Month

❑ International Strategic Thinking Month
Free Chess Game with Every Purchase

❑ Library Card Sign Up Month

❑ Menopause Awareness Month

❑ Metaphysical Awareness Month
Our Prices Are Great on Every Plane!

❑ National Biscuit Month

❑ National Chicken Month

❑ National Coupon Month
Have You Seen Our Flyer?

❑ National 5-A-Day Month

❑ National Food Allergy Awareness Month

❑ National Home School Month

❑ National Honey Month
Come in for Sweet Deals!

❑ National Little League Month

❑ National Mushroom Month

❑ National Organic Harvest Month
Nothing Artificial About These Low Prices

❑ National Piano Month

- ❑ National Potato Month
- ❑ National Rice Month
- ❑ National School Success Month
- ❑ National Very Important Parents (VIP) Month
- ❑ National Skin Care Awareness Month
- ❑ Pleasure Your Mate Month
- ❑ Sea Cadet Month
- ❑ Self-Improvement Month
- ❑ Healthy Aging Month
- ❑ Shameless Promotion Month *Trust Us— Our Sales Are GREAT!*
- ❑ Southern Gospel Music Month
- ❑ Subliminal Communications Month
- ❑ United Planet Month *Imports for Less!*
- ❑ Update Your Resume Month
- ❑ National Hispanic Heritage Month
- ❑ National Hot Rod Association US Nationals
- ❑ US Open
- ❑ Oslo Marathon
- ❑ Maryland Crabs & Corn Festival
- ❑ Nashville Greek Festival
- ❑ New York's Chocolate Show
- ❑ America's Farm Aid
- ❑ Bicycle Messenger World Championships

Promotions & Events
To Celebrate For September By Week

- ❑ International Enthusiasm Week . . . . September 1-7
- ❑ National Childhood Injury Prevention Week . . . . September 1-7
- ❑ Self-University Week. . . . . September 1-7

- ❏ National Waffle Week . . . . September 4-10
- ❏ Play Days . . . . September 6-10
- ❏ Bald Is Beautiful Days . . . . September 9-11
- ❏ National Emergency Preparedness Week . . . . September 11-17
  Stock Up on Supplies!
- ❏ National No Bully Week . . . . September 12-16
- ❏ Love a Mensch Week . . . . September 12-18
- ❏ Constitution Week . . . . September 17-23
- ❏ Build a Better Image Week . . . . September 18-24
- ❏ Deaf Awareness Week . . . . September 18-24
- ❏ Balance Awareness Week . . . . September 18-24
- ❏ National Dog Week . . . . September 18-24
- ❏ National Farm Animals Awareness Week . . . . September 18-24
- ❏ National Farm & Ranch Safety & Health Week . . . . September 18-24
- ❏ National Historically Black College Week . . . . September 18-24
- ❏ Tolkien Week . . . . September 18-24
  One Ring to Make Her Smile
- ❏ National Baby Safety Week . . . . September 19-25
- ❏ Lunch Prowl Week . . . . September 20-24
- ❏ Religious Freedom Week . . . . September 23-October 2
- ❏ National Chimney Safety Week. . . . . September 24-30
- ❏ Banned Books Week . . . . September 24-October 1

❑ Chicken Boy's Day . . . . September 1

❑ Emma M. Nutt Day . . . . September 1

❑ Bison-Ten-Yell Day . . . . September 2

❑ Newspaper Carrier Day . . . . September 4

❑ Be Late for Something Day . . . . September 5

❑ Buhl Day . . . . September 5

❑ Labor Day . . . . September 5

❑ Another Look Unlimited Day . . . . September 6

❑ Do It! Day . . . . September 6

❑ Google Commemoration Day . . . . September 7

❑ Grandma Moses Day . . . . September 7

❑ National Feel the Love Day . . . . September 7

❑ International Literacy Day . . . . September 8

❑ Wonderful Weirdos Day . . . . September 9

❑ Sew Be It! Day . . . . September 10
Sew Up the Savings!

❑ Swap Ideas Day . . . . September 10

❑ Patriot Day . . . . September 11
Red, White, and Blue Promotions

❑ Remember Freedom Day . . . . September 11

SEPTEMBER

WORLD
TOURISM
DAY

Birthdays To Celebrate In September
(Can be used for either price or non price promotions)

❏ Dr. Phil McGraw. . . . . September 1

❏ Beyonce Knowles. . . . . September 4

❏ Jeff Foxworthy . . . . September 6

❏ Pink . . . . September 8

❏ Adam Sandler. . . . . September 9

❏ Ludacris . . . . September 11

❏ Tommy Lee Jones . . . . September 15

❏ Prince Harry . . . . September 15

❏ BB King . . . . September 16

❏ Nicole Richie . . . . September 21

❏ Faith Hill. . . . . September 21

❏ Stephen King . . . . September 21
   We Have a Horror of High Prices!

❏ Jim Henson . . . . September 24

❏ Will Smith . . . . September 25

❏ Mark Hamill . . . . September 25

❏ Barbara Walters . . . . September 25

❏ George Gershwin . . . . September 26

❏ Hilary Duff. . . . . September 28

**More reasons to promote can be found
in Chase's Calendar of Events.**

NOTES

OCTOBER

Is the thought of running out of promotional ideas scaring you? Don't be afraid! With Columbus Day and Halloween in October, plenty of sales tactics present themselves to retailers of every stripe. Special days for NASCAR fans, mystery lovers, animal fanatics and parents also present many marketing opportunities through the month.

Classic October Sale Terms

- ❏ Bite Into Savings
- ❏ Boo-dacious Bargains
- ❏ Cellar Dweller Deals
- ❏ Columbus Day Sailing Savings
- ❏ Columbus Day Weekend
- ❏ Dangerously Unstable Prices
- ❏ Devilish Deals a Halloween Spooktacular!
- ❏ A Nine Inning Sale
- ❏ A Treat So Cool It's Scary
- ❏ Add the Extras for Free
- ❏ After Midnight
- ❏ All the Best, All for Less
- ❏ Autumn Color Accent

- ❏ Be Afraid. Be Very Afraid.
- ❏ Be Safe Be Seen on Halloween
- ❏ Best of Fall
- ❏ Bewitching Bargains! Bewitching Buys! Bewitching Savings!
- ❏ Biggest Sale Ever
- ❏ Dig Our Discounts
- ❏ Discover a World of Savings
- ❏ Discover the Great Columbus Day Sales Extravaganza
- ❏ Discovery Day
- ❏ Don't Miss the Boat on Columbus Day Savings!
- ❏ Don't Pay Til Next Year

- ❏ Everything Below Sticker Price
- ❏ Eye-Popping Tricks and Treats
- ❏ Fall Clean-Up
- ❏ Fall Colors
- ❏ Fall Family Fest
- ❏ Fall Fashion Week
- ❏ Fall Fest
- ❏ Fall Festival
- ❏ Fall Festival of Leaves
- ❏ Fall Fiesta
- ❏ Fall Furniture Extravaganza
- ❏ Fall Home Festival
- ❏ Fall in Love All Over Again
- ❏ Fall Into a Great
- ❏ Fall Into Fashion
- ❏ Fall Into Our
- ❏ Fall Lawn & Garden
- ❏ Fall Savings Stock Up
- ❏ Fill Your Sails with Columbus Day Sales
- ❏ First Snow Sale
- ❏ Fourth and Long Bargains
- ❏ Freaky Friday

- ❏ Fright Night Fashion
- ❏ Frightfully Good Deals
- ❏ Fun for Little Monsters
- ❏ Get Here Early
- ❏ Get It All Here
- ❏ Get It, Got It, Good
- ❏ Get Stoked at Our Wood Stove Spectacular
- ❏ Goblin Alert
- ❏ Got Candy? Lots of Candy?
- ❏ Great Gridiron Days Grills
- ❏ Halloween Madness
- ❏ Hard Bargains on Software
- ❏ Haunted House Sale
- ❏ Have a Little Mercy
- ❏ Holiday Coupon
- ❏ Howling Great Deals
- ❏ Hunt Down Low Prices
- ❏ If It's in the Rainbow, It's Reduced
- ❏ If It's Sweet, It's on Sale
- ❏ Isn't This Something?
- ❏ Killer Prices Sale

- ❑ Last Minute Sale
- ❑ Leaf Peepers Welcome
- ❑ Midnight Madness
- ❑ Monster Sale
- ❑ Monster Mash Sales Bash
- ❑ Mummies Love Our Prices
- ❑ Nine Innings of Savings
- ❑ Noon to Night
- ❑ Not for the Faint of Heart
- ❑ Not for the Timid
- ❑ October Thank You Days
- ❑ Off Our Rocker Sale
- ❑ Oktoberfest Specials
- ❑ Our Prices Are So Low It's Scary!
- ❑ Prices Are Falling
- ❑ Prices Are Falling with the Leaves
- ❑ Rediscover America's Values
- ❑ So Many Choices
- ❑ Spooktacular Family Fun!
- ❑ Start Your Journey with Us
- ❑ Suggested Prices Are for Losers
- ❑ The Bargains Only Come Out at Night
- ❑ The Height of Fright
- ❑ The Most Bone Chilling Sale I've Seen in a Decade
- ❑ Un-boo-lievable Halloween Bargains
- ❑ Well Below Retail
- ❑ We're Afraid…of Our Own Prices
- ❑ We've Scared Up Some Savings
- ❑ Yes, Folks, It Has Frozen Over
- ❑ You'll Be Shocked at the Savings
- ❑ Your Ship Has Come in… Loaded with Bargains
- ❑ Zip Up a Package Deal

Promotions & Events
To Celebrate For October

- ❏ Adopt a Shelter Dog Month
- ❏ Alternate History Month
- ❏ Animals Aloud! Month
- ❏ Billiard Awareness Month
- ❏ Celebrate Sun Dried Tomatoes Month
- ❏ Children's Magazine Month
- ❏ Diversity Awareness Month
  A Different Sale for Everybody!
- ❏ Eat Better, Eat Together Month
- ❏ Emotional Wellness Month
- ❏ Gay and Lesbian History Month
- ❏ Go Hog Wild – Eat Country Ham Month
- ❏ Halloween Safety Month
- ❏ Head Start Awareness Month
- ❏ Health Literacy Month
- ❏ International Starman Month
- ❏ National Book Month
  Best Sellers for Less!
- ❏ National Breast Cancer Awareness Month
- ❏ National Chili Month
- ❏ National Communicate with Your Kids Month
  Buy One Cell Phone, Get One Free!
- ❏ National Construction Toy Month
- ❏ National Cookie Month
- ❏ National Crime Prevention Month
- ❏ National Dental Hygiene Mouth
- ❏ National Popcorn Poppin' Month
- ❏ National Pork Month
- ❏ National Reading Group Month
  Buy Three Books, Get Three Free!
- ❏ National Roller Skating Month
- ❏ National Seafood Month
- ❏ October Is Discover America Month
- ❏ Polish American Heritage Month

- ❏ Positive Attitude Month
- ❏ Right Brainers Rule! Month
- ❏ Self-Promotion Month
- ❏ Spinach Lovers Month
- ❏ Vegetarian Month
- ❏ Women's Small Business Month
- ❏ World Series

- ❏ Ironman Triathalon
- ❏ Cingular Wireless Bayou Boogaloo & Cajun Food Festival
- ❏ San Francisco Fringe Festival
- ❏ Oktoberfest
- ❏ San Gennaro Feast Days

Promotions & Events
To Celebrate For October By Week

- ❏ Universal Children's Week . . . . October 1-7
- ❏ No Salt Week . . . . October 2-6
- ❏ Mystery Series Week . . . . October 2-8
- ❏ National Carry a Tune Week . . . . October 2-8
  Sing for Your Savings!
- ❏ National Newspaper Week . . . . October 2-8
- ❏ Squirrel Appreciation Week . . . . October 2-8
  Our Prices Are So Low We Must Be Nuts!
- ❏ California Ride Share Week . . . . October 3-7
- ❏ Spinning and Weaving Week . . . . October 3-7
- ❏ World Space Week . . . . October 4-10
- ❏ Emergency Nurses Week . . . . October 9-15

❑ Fire Prevention Week . . . . October 9-15
Can You Put a Price on Safety?

❑ National Metric Week . . . . October 9-15

❑ Home Based Business Week . . . . October 9-15

❑ National School Lunch Week . . . . October 9-15

❑ Improve Your Home Office Week . . . . October 10-14

❑ Kids Care Week . . . . October 16-22

❑ Teen Read Week . . . . October 16-22

❑ National Character Counts Week . . . . October 16-22

❑ National Chemistry Week . . . . October 16-22

❑ National Food Bank Week . . . . October 16-22

❑ National Forest Products Week . . . . October 16-22

❑ Freedom From Bullies at Work Week . . . . October 17-23

❑ National Businesswomen's Week . . . . October 17-23

❑ World Rainforest Week . . . . October 17-23

❑ Celebrate Job Loss Week . . . . October 23-29

❑ Give Wildlife a Break Week . . . . October 23-29

❑ The Magic of Differences Week . . . . October 23-29

❑ National Save Your Back Week . . . . October 23-29

❑ Pastoral Care Week . . . . October 23-29

❑ Peace, Friendship and Goodwill Week . . . . October 25-31

Promotions & Events
To Celebrate For October By Day

- ❏ Fire Pup Day. . . . . October 1
- ❏ International Day of Older Person . . . . October 1
- ❏ International Frugal Fun Day . . . . October 1
- ❏ Pumpkin Day . . . . October 1
- ❏ Scare a Friend Day . . . . October 1
- ❏ World Vegetarian Day . . . . October 1
- ❏ National Custodial Workers Day . . . . October 2
- ❏ World Farm Animals Day . . . . October 2
- ❏ Intergeneration Day . . . . October 2
- ❏ Child Health Day . . . . October 3
- ❏ Supreme Court Day . . . . October 3
- ❏ World Habitat Day . . . . October 3
- ❏ Ten-Four Day . . . . October 4
- ❏ Toot Your Flute Day . . . . October 4
- ❏ Balloons Around the World . . . . October 5
- ❏ National German-American Day . . . . October 6
- ❏ National Diversity Day . . . . October 7
- ❏ World Smile Day . . . . October 7
- ❏ Back to Basics Day . . . . October 8
- ❏ Leif Erickson Day . . . . October 9

OCTOBER

OCTOBER

National
Magic Day

Birthdays To Celebrate In October
(Can be used for either price or non price promotions)

❑ Julie Andrews. . . . . October 1

❑ Kelly Ripa . . . . October 2

❑ Sting . . . . October 2

❑ Stevie Ray Vaughan . . . . October 3
   Great for Guitar Sales

❑ Susan Sarandon . . . . October 4

❑ Anne Rice . . . . October 4

❑ Vladimir Putin . . . . October 7

❑ Simon Cowell . . . . October 7
   Have an "American Idol" Event

❑ Chevy Chase . . . . October 8

❑ RL Stine . . . . October 8
   A Sale So Good We Get Goosebumps!

❑ Dale Earnhardt, Jr. . . . . October 10

❑ Eleanor Roosevelt . . . . October 11

❑ Margaret Thatcher . . . . October 13

❑ Usher. . . . . October 14

❑ Ralph Lauren . . . . October 14

❑ Emeril Lagasse . . . . October 15

❑ Oscar Wilde . . . . October 16

❑ Eminem . . . . October 17

❑ Alan Jackson . . . . October 17

❑ Martina Navratilova . . . . October 18

❑ Mike Ditka. . . . . October 18
   All Bears Memorabilia on Sale!

❑ Snoop Dogg. . . . . October 20

❑ Bela Lugosi . . . . October 20

❑ Judge Judy Sheindlin . . . . October 21

❑ Johnny Carson . . . . October 23

❑ Pablo Picasso . . . . October 25

❑ Hillary Rodham Clinton . . . . October 26

❑ Roberto Benigni . . . . October 27

❑ Julia Roberts . . . . October 28

❑ Bill Gates . . . . October 28
   *Buy a Computer, We'll Throw in a Bundled
   Operating System for Free!*

❑ Jane Pauley . . . . October 31

**Need more dates? Check out
Chase's Calendar of Events**

NOTES

NOVEMBER

It's the most wonderful time of the year! With early Christmas shoppers, Thanksgiving, Veteran's Day, and pre-season winter promotions to run, you might not think you need another reason to have a sale. But in case you do, we've got some great ones, including Military Family Appreciation Day – great to tie to your Veteran's Day celebrations – and National Fun With Fondue Month.

Classic November Sale Terms

- ❏ _____Shopping Days Till Christmas!
- ❏ A Harvest of Healthy Savings
- ❏ After Thanksgiving Sale Starts Tomorrow
- ❏ All I Want for Christmas Is on Sale At
- ❏ All the Trimmings
- ❏ All Time Favorites for Your Thanksgiving Feast
- ❏ Are You Ready for Winter?
- ❏ Beat the December Rush
- ❏ Best of Fall
- ❏ Black Friday Blowout!

- ❏ Dash in for Christmas Specials
- ❏ Dear Santa
- ❏ Deck the Halls with Holiday Deals
- ❏ Don't Be a Turkey
- ❏ Early Snowbird Sale
- ❏ Even Santa Shops Here
- ❏ Feast on These Savings
- ❏ From Santa's Elves to Our Shelves…Fabulous Christmas Gifts
- ❏ Get Your Taste Buds Ready
- ❏ Get Stuffed with Savings

- ❏ Gobble, Gobble, Gobble Up the Values!
- ❏ Gotta Have It? We've Got It!
- ❏ Great Gridiron Days Grills
- ❏ Great Stocking Stuffers
- ❏ Harvest Sale
- ❏ Ho! Ho! Ho! Our Prices Are Low, Low, Low!
- ❏ Holiday Season Kick-Off
- ❏ Home for the Holiday
- ❏ Honor the Great Ones
- ❏ Hot Toys Here!
- ❏ How to Wrap Up a Sale
- ❏ Humbugs Aren't Invited
- ❏ I Thought a Quarterback Was a Big Sale
- ❏ In a Blaze of Glory Veteran's Day Sale
- ❏ In December, You'll Be Glad You Thought of It Now
- ❏ It's Toy Time...Are You Ready?
- ❏ It's Flu Season...So Come Empty Our Coffers
- ❏ Kick Off the Season with Our
- ❏ Layaway for Christmas Now
- ❏ Layaway for Later

- ❏ Let's Talk Turkey
- ❏ Magic of Lights
- ❏ Make the Most of Your Christmas Dollars
- ❏ Mercury's Falling...So Are Our Prices!
- ❏ Miles of Smiles
- ❏ Need a Little Christmas
- ❏ No Scrooges Allowed
- ❏ November Countdown to the Holidays
- ❏ November Is Novice Month – Get Lessons for Less
- ❏ Oh, What Fun It Is to Buy!
- ❏ Ol' Man Winter's On His Way
- ❏ Only You Know What You Want
- ❏ Play It Safe...Shop Early
- ❏ Pre-Christmas Selection, After Christmas Prices!
- ❏ Pre-Season Spectacular!
- ❏ Pre-Winter Energy
- ❏ Pre-Winter Sale Is on Now
- ❏ Santa Knows Where the Savings Are
- ❏ Santa Will Sleigh You
- ❏ Santa's Sack

- ❏ Santa's Super Saving Specials!
- ❏ Savings You Can Truly Be Thankful For
- ❏ Savor Our Tasty Bargains
- ❏ Season of Joy
- ❏ Season of Sharing
- ❏ Season's Greetings
- ❏ See Santa and Save
- ❏ See the Game with Us
- ❏ Share Your Secrets with Santa
- ❏ Shop Early and Save
- ❏ Snow Days Discounts
- ❏ Stock the Fridge
- ❏ Stock Up for Winter
- ❏ Stock Up on Slow Food
- ❏ Stocking Stuffer
- ❏ Thanks-For-Giving
- ❏ Thanksgiving Marathon Sales Event
- ❏ The Home of the Brave Sales Event
- ❏ The Ultimate Ski Sale
- ❏ The Winter Shoe & Boot Blowout
- ❏ There's No Time Like the Present for Presents
- ❏ Think Thanksgiving
- ❏ This Year's Hottest Gifts
- ❏ To Give Is Human, to Save Divine
- ❏ Too Many Cooks Mean Even More Savings
- ❏ Top Gift Ideas
- ❏ "Twas the Sale Before Christmas
- ❏ Veteran's Day Parade of Savings
- ❏ We Won't Tell Them It Was on Sale
- ❏ We're So Stoked – Fireplace Prices Have Fallen
- ❏ We're Your Secret Santa
- ❏ We've Got What's on Your List at Santa's Sidewalk
- ❏ What Are You Waiting For?
- ❏ When It Snows You Save
- ❏ While They're Watching Football…
- ❏ Winter Starts Soon! Are You Ready?
- ❏ Winter Weatherizing
- ❏ Workey Off the Turkey
- ❏ You'll Need a Bigger Stocking
- ❏ Yule Find It Here!

Promotions & Events
To Celebrate For November

- Aviation History Month
- Cozy Cuddles for Kids Month
- Family Stories Month
  Capture the Memories!
- I Am So Thankful Month
- International Drum Month
- Military Family Appreciation Month
- National Adoption Month
- National American Indian Heritage Month
- National Author's Day Month
- National Family Caregivers Month
- National Fun with Fondue Month
- National Georgia Pecans Month
- National Healthy Skin Month
- National Life Writing Month
- National Peanut Butter Lovers Month
  Prices So Low They're Nuts!
- Vegan Month
- Cut Your Own Christmas Tree Month
- Country Music Awards
- NASCAR Nextel Cup
- Melbourne Cup
- New York City Marathon
- Florida Pirate Festival
- Macy's Thanksgiving Day Parade
- North Carolina International Festival
- Elephant Pumpkin Stomp at the National Zoo

National Peanut Butter Lovers Month

Promotions & Events
To Celebrate For November By Week

❑ National Fig Week . . . . November 1-7

❑ World Communication Week . . . . November 1-7

❑ Dear Santa Letter Week . . . . November 1-7

❑ Synergy Week . . . . .November 6-12

❑ Kids' Goal Setting Week . . . . .November 7-11

❑ World Kindness Week .November 7-13

❑ National Animal Shelter Appreciation . . . . .November 7-13

❑ Pursuit of Happiness Week . . . . .November 8-14
   You Can't Buy Happiness…or Can You?

❑ Great American Warm-Up Days . . . . November 11-13

❑ American Education Week . . . . November 13-19

❑ Children's Book Week . . . . November 14-20
   Come to Our Local Author Signing!

❑ National Farm-City Week . . . . November 18-24

❑ National Adoption Week . . . . November 20-26

❑ National Family Week . . . . November 20-26

❑ National Game and Puzzle Week. . . . . November 20-26

❑ Better Conversation Week. . . . . November 21-27
   Our Sales Are Something Worth Talking About!

Promotions & Events
To Celebrate For November By Day

- ❑ National Author's Day . . . . .November 1

- ❑ National Family Literacy Day . . . . .November 1
  Buy a Book for Mom, Get Two for the Kids!

- ❑ Election Day . . . . .November 2

- ❑ National Traffic Director's Day. . . . . .November 2
  Pick a Straight Route to Savings!

- ❑ Plan Your Epitaph Day . . . . .November 2
  We Suggest 'He Died Happy!'

- ❑ Cliché Day . . . . .November 3

- ❑ National Men Make Dinner Day . . . . .November 3

- ❑ Sandwich Day . . . . .November 3

- ❑ National Chicken Lady Day . . . . .November 4

- ❑ Sadie Hawkins Day . . . . .November 5

- ❑ Gingerbread House Day . . . . .November 7

- ❑ Abet and Aid Punsters Day . . . . .November 8
  Enter Our Pun Contest!

- ❑ Cook Something Bold & Pungent Day . . . . .November 8

- ❑ National Parents as Teachers Day. . . . . .November 8

- ❑ X-Ray Day . . . . .November 8
  See Through to Savings!

- ❑ National Young Readers Day . . . . .November 9

- ❑ Vietnam Veterans Memorial Day . . . . .November 9

❏ You're Welcomegiving Day . . . . November 25

❏ Flossing Day . . . . November 25

❏ International Aura Awareness Day . . . . November 26

❏ Electronic Greetings Day . . . . November 29

❏ Computer Security Day . . . . November 30

❏ Stay Home Because You're Well Day . . . . November 30

Birthdays To Celebrate In November
(Can be used for either price or non price promotions)

❏ Jenny McCarthy . . . . November 1

❏ Nelly . . . . November 2

❏ Marie Antoinette . . . . November 2
   Off with High Prices!

❏ Dennis Miller . . . . November 3

❏ Sean "Diddy" Combs . . . . November 4

❏ Laura Bush . . . . November 4

❏ Sally Field . . . . November 6
   You Like Us, You Really Like Us!

❏ Nich Lachey . . . . November 9

❏ George Patton . . . . November 11
   Great Veteran's Day Tie-In*

❏ Whoopi Goldberg . . . . November 13

- [ ] Prince Charles . . . . November 14
- [ ] Jodie Foster . . . . November 19
- [ ] Rodney Dangerfield . . . . November 22
  You've Gotta Respect Low Prices!
- [ ] Ben Stein . . . . November 25
- [ ] Jon Stewart . . . . November 28
- [ ] Ben Stiller . . . . November 30
- [ ] Dick Clark . . . . November 30

**Need more dates? Check out
Chase's Calendar of Events!**

NOTES

DECEMBER

Of all the months, December features the fewest offbeat or unusual celebrations. Most of the time and energy is devoted to Christmas – but if you're desperate for something different, we've dug up a few gems for you!

Classic December Sale Terms

- ❑ A New Look for a New Year
- ❑ A Smart Start for a New Year
- ❑ A Very Merry After-Christmas Sale
- ❑ A Winter Sale You'll Warm Up To
- ❑ After All, This Sale Is All Downhill
- ❑ After Christmas Sale Starts Today!
- ❑ Ball-Dropping Bargains
- ❑ Before You Hit Mountains, Hit Our Ski Sale
- ❑ Blizzard Blowout Sale
- ❑ Boys of Summer Winter Event

- ❑ Boys Toys
- ❑ Bring Home the Magic of Christmas
- ❑ Buy Yourself a Gift This Christmas
- ❑ Capture the Moment
- ❑ Christmas Comes But Once a Year
- ❑ Christmas Is a Wrap
- ❑ Cross-Country Ski Sale
- ❑ Dash In for Christmas Specials
- ❑ Dashing Through the Values
- ❑ Days After Christmas
- ❑ December Sales If It Snows Days
- ❑ Deck the Hall with Holiday Values

- ❏ Don't Blame Us If You Miss It
- ❏ Don't Pay Till Next Year
- ❏ Down the Chimney
- ❏ Dress Your Windows for Winter
- ❏ Dynamite Winter Clearance
- ❏ Early Bird Specials... Doors Open At
- ❏ End of the Year Sales Spectacular
- ❏ Even Santa Saves At...
- ❏ Even Santa Shops Here
- ❏ Festival of Lights
- ❏ Fill Your List in Minutes
- ❏ Get a New Start Sales Event
- ❏ Get Here Early
- ❏ Get It All Here
- ❏ Got Everything?
- ❏ Got the Jingle Bell Blues?
- ❏ Holiday Dazzle
- ❏ Holiday Glamour
- ❏ Holiday Hangover
- ❏ Holiday Wrap Up Sale

- ❏ Hurry! There's Only _____ Days Left
- ❏ Imagine Their Faces
- ❏ Last Call for Christmas
- ❏ Last Minute Christmas Buys
- ❏ Last Minute Sale
- ❏ Last Time This Year
- ❏ Leave the Wrapping to Us...Free Gift Wrapping with Purchase
- ❏ Let's End _____ with a Blast
- ❏ Make Her Speechless
- ❏ Make Room for Next Year
- ❏ Making Space Sale
- ❏ Mark Down Madness Sale
- ❏ Midnight Madness
- ❏ Need a Little Christmas
- ❏ Now Through New Year's Day
- ❏ Open Early
- ❏ Our Discounts Will Sleigh You
- ❏ Our Very-Merry After Christmas Sale
- ❏ Out with the Old
- ❏ Presents for Your Princess

- ❏ Ring In the New Year
- ❏ Ring Out the Old and Ring In the New with _____
- ❏ Santa Can't Forget
- ❏ Santa's Cleared for Takeoff!
- ❏ Santa's Helper Works Here
- ❏ Santa's Secret Stash
- ❏ Santa's Sidewalk Sale
- ❏ Save Like Scrooge
- ❏ Season Ending Blowout
- ❏ Secret Santa Deals
- ❏ Sleighful of Savings
- ❏ Start the New Year Off Right
- ❏ Start the New Year with a Smile
- ❏ Take Her Breath Away
- ❏ The Christmas Countdown
- ❏ The Sale You've Been Waiting For
- ❏ The Season Is the Reason
- ❏ The Twelve Days of Christmas Promotion
- ❏ This Year's Hottest Gifts
- ❏ Time Is Running Out Sale
- ❏ Tis the Season to Save
- ❏ Toys for Big Boys
- ❏ Trim a Tree Buys
- ❏ Trust Us, She Doesn't Really Want a Vacuum
- ❏ Under the Wire Last Sale
- ❏ Warm Up to Our Winter Bargains
- ❏ We Need the Space
- ❏ We Saved The Best Sale for Last
- ❏ We Wish You a Merry Christmas
- ❏ Who Needs Christmas Wrap in January
- ❏ Winter Carnival
- ❏ Winter Luau
- ❏ Winter Madness
- ❏ Wrap Up the Holiday
- ❏ Year's Up! Prices Are Down!
- ❏ Year-End Countdown Sell-A-Thon
- ❏ Year-End Sell-Off
- ❏ Yule Tide Savings

DECEMBER

Promotions & Events
To Celebrate For December

- ❏ Bingo's Birthday Month

- ❏ National Stress-Free
  Holidays Month
  We've Made Shopping Easy!

- ❏ National Tie Month

- ❏ Safe Toys and Gifts Month

- ❏ Read a New Book Month

- ❏ Spiritual Literacy Month

- ❏ Universal Human
  Rights Month

Promotions & Events
To Celebrate For December By Week

- ❏ Cookie Cutter Week . . . . December 1-7
  Baking Promotions

- ❏ Tolerance Week . . . . December 1-7

- ❏ Recipe Greetings for the Holidays . . . . December 1-8

- ❏ Human Rights Week . . . . .December 4-10

- ❏ International Language Week . . . . December 15-21

- ❏ It's About Time Week. . . . . .December 25-31

Promotions & Events
To Celebrate For December By Day

❑ Bifocals at the Monitor Liberation Day . . . . December 1

❑ Day Without Art Day . . . . December 1
  Prints and Poster Sale!

❑ Safety Razor Day . . . . December 2

❑ Coats for Kids Day . . . . December 3

❑ National Dice Day . . . . December 4

❑ Bathtub Party Day . . . . December 5

❑ National Communicate with Your Kids Day . . . . December 6

❑ St. Nicholas Day . . . . December 6

❑ National Pearl Harbor Remembrance Day . . . . December 7

❑ Human Rights Day . . . . December 10

❑ Nobel Prize Awards Day . . . . December 10

❑ Day of the Horse . . . . December 10

❑ Wright Brothers Day . . . . December 17

❑ Underdog Day . . . . December 17

❑ Mudd Day . . . . December 20

❑ Forefathers Day . . . . December 21

❑ Humbug Day . . . . December 21

❑ Phileas Fogg Win a Wager Day . . . . December 21

❑ World Peace Day . . . . December 21

❑ Winter Solstice . . . . December 21

- ❏ A'Phabet Day (No "L" Day) . . . . December 25
- ❏ Boxing Day . . . . December 26
- ❏ National Whiner's Day . . . . December 26
- ❏ Tick Tock Day . . . . December 29
  It's Time for a New Clock!
- ❏ No Interruptions Day . . . . December 29
- ❏ International Walk Day . . . . December 30
- ❏ Leap Second Time Adjustment Day . . . . December 31
- ❏ Make Up Your Mind Day . . . . December 31
- ❏ World Peace Meditation Day . . . . December 31
- ❏ New Year's Eve . . . . December 31

Birthdays To Celebrate In December
(Can be used for either price or non price promotions)

- ❏ Woody Allen . . . . .December 1
- ❏ Richard Pryor . . . . .December 1
- ❏ Britney Spears . . . . .December 2
- ❏ Gianni Versace . . . . .December 2
  Get the Look for Less!
- ❏ Ozzy Osbourne . . . . .December 3
- ❏ Tyra Banks . . . . .December 4
- ❏ Jay-Z . . . . .December 4
- ❏ Walt Disney . . . . .December 5
  Deep Disney Discounts!

DECEMBER

Need more dates? Check out Chase's Calendar of Events!

NOTES

About the Author
Rick Segel

A seasoned retailer of 25 years, Rick Segel, CSP (Certified Speaking Professional), is an international award-winning speaker, author, trainer, and consultant, who has delivered over 1,700 presentations on three continents and in 47 states. He is a contributing writer for numerous national and international publications and a founding member of the Retail Advisory Council for Johnson & Wales University, Providence, R.I. Rick is Director of Retail Training for the Retailers Association of Massachusetts and the creator of the RAMAES, an awards program that honors outstanding Massachusetts retailers. He is also the on-line marketing expert for Staples.com.

Rick has authored five audio programs, two training videos, and eight books, including the #1 best-selling *Retail Business Kit for Dummies*. His book *Laugh & Get Rich*, published by Specific House, has been critically acclaimed as a must-read for its insightful outlook at our entertainment-based society, and has been translated into Japanese, Chinese, and Korean. He has appeared on more than 100 radio and TV shows, including *Sally Jesse Raphael*.

For more information about Rick Segel, please visit www.ricksegel.com.

EDUCATIONAL PRODUCTS FOR
RETAIL & SMALL BUSINESS

As a seasoned retailer and retail consultant, Rick Segel has created a number of resources for retailers that are packed with practical techniques and useful knowledge. These resources cover such topics as improving sales conversion rates, suggestive selling, achieving profitability, running a sale and becoming a preferred vendor. These are also resources that teach you techniques for starting and running retail businesses. Visit **www.RickSegel.com**, take your time and browse through our products. You can purchase any of our products using our secure on-line shopping cart.

www.RickSegel.com